Logistics Management

MARKET LEADER

Business English

Nina O'Driscoll and Adrian Pilbeam

PEARSON
Longman

FINANCIAL
TIMES

Pearson Education Limited

Pearson Education Limited
Edinburgh Gate
Harlow
Essex CM20 2JE
England
and Associated Companies throughout the world.

www.pearsonlongman.com

© Pearson Education Limited 2010

The right of Nina O'Driscoll and Adrian Pilbeam to be identified as authors of this Work has been asserted by them in accordance with the Copyright, Designs and Patents Act 1988.

First published 2010

ISBN 978-1-408-22006-1

Set in Metaplus, Times & ITC Cheltenham
Printed in Great Britian by Ashford Colour Press Ltd.

Acknowledgements

This series was developed and written by consultants working with LTS Training and Consulting, Bath, a specialist language and intercultural training company.

The authors and publishers are grateful to the following teachers who reported on earlier drafts of this material: Aukjen Bosma and Christine Thuillier.

Adrian Pilbeam would like to thank the many specialists in logistics and supply-chain management from leading European companies with whom he has worked on training courses over the last five years and from whom he has learned much about the crucial role of the supply chain in international business.

We are grateful to the following for permission to reproduce copyright material:

Text

Extracts in Units 3, 6 and 14 from *Logistics and Supply Chain Management – Creating Value-Adding Networks*, 3rd edition, Financial Times/Prentice Hall (Christopher, M. 2005) copyright © Pearson Education Limited; Extract in Unit 10 adapted from 'A very tight supply chain', *Financial Times*, 27 March 2007 (Murray, S.), copyright © Sarah Murray; Extract in Unit 17 adapted from 'Green supply chains: moving beyond logistics', *Financial Times*, 10 December 2007 (Murray, S.), copyright © Sarah Murray.

The Financial Times

Extract in Unit 1 adapted from 'Supplying a new demand', *The Financial Times*, 21 August 2008 (Birchall, J.), copyright © Financial Times Ltd; Extract in Unit 7 adapted from 'Silver lining to high oil prices', *The Financial Times*, 30 July 2008 (De Meyer, A. and Holweg, M.), copyright © Financial Times Ltd; Extract in Unit 8 adapted from 'Foreign makers find advantages on more familiar turf', *The Financial Times*, 8 May 2006 (Marsh, P.), copyright © Financial Times Ltd; Extract in Unit 9 adapted from 'Moral maze for retailers reliant on developing world suppliers', *The Financial Times*, 2 July 2008, copyright © Financial Times Ltd; Extract in Unit 11 adapted from 'Oil price forces P&G to rethink its distribution', *The Financial Times*, 27 June 2008 (Birchall, J. and Rigby, E.), copyright © Financial Times Ltd; Extract in Unit 15 adapted from 'Inventory: RFID – the price must be right', *The Financial Times*, 30 May 2006 (Blau, J.), copyright © Financial Times Ltd; Extract in Unit 16 adapted from 'Jaguar Land Rover: "milk run" is miles better', *The Financial Times*, 9 October 2008 (Newing, R.), copyright © Financial Times Ltd; Extract in Unit 18 adapted from 'Demands spread along the supply chain', *The Financial Times*, 7 November 2007 (Ilett, D.), copyright © Financial Times Ltd.

Photos

The publisher would like to thank the following for their kind permission to reproduce their photographs:

(Key: b-bottom; c-centre; l-left; r-right; t-top)

Alamy Images: Julio Etchart 33, Images-USA 45, Richard Levine 9, SHOUT 21, Sue Cunningham Photographic 29, Colin Underhill 65; **Corbis**: Louie Psihoyos 5, George Steinmetz 25; **Getty Images**: Mario Villafuerte 53; **iStockphoto**: 41, 61tr, Greenstock 49, Johannes Norpoth 69, Joe Tamassy 61tl; **Jupiter Unlimited**: Stockxpert 61br; **Pearson Education Royalty-Free/Commissioned**: Photodisc 17; **Photolibrary.com**: Image Source 3; **Reuters**: STR New 37, Bobby Yip 73; **Rex Features**: Francis Dean 13, Alex Segre 57

Cover photo © Getty Images: Thierry Dosogne

Project managed by Chris Hartley

Contents

The importance of an efficient supply chain

This unit explains why an efficient supply chain is important for the success and profitability of a company.

BEFORE YOU READ

Discuss these questions.

1 How would you define a *supply chain*?
2 What makes a supply chain efficient?
3 What problems can be caused when a supply chain does not work efficiently?
4 How would you define *vertically integrated production*?
5 What do you understand by *tier-one suppliers*? And what are *tier-two*, *tier-three* or *tier-four suppliers*?

READING

A Understanding the main points

Read the article on the opposite page and answer these questions.

1 What kinds of company already have efficient supply chains?
2 Why is having an effective supply chain so important, especially in this period of globalisation?
3 What can be the result of supply-chain problems?
4 Which industry sectors have less-developed supply chains?
5 When does the supply chain become especially critical for manufacturers?
6 Why is supply-chain management so important to the aerospace industry?

B Understanding details

Read the article again and answer these questions.

1 Why is an efficient supply chain a prize worth working for?
2 Why is it difficult for consumer goods and retailing companies to make improvements to their supply chains?
3 Give two examples of what can result from mistakes in the supply chain of retailing companies.
4 Who does Hewlett-Packard's supply chain expert need to communicate with in its supply chain?
5 What do supply-chain managers increasingly need from their supply chains?
6 What two examples are given of unexpected problems that can affect a supply chain?
7 Why is improving the supply chain such a challenge for the aerospace and defence industries?
8 What is the cost of a large modern aircraft?
9 Why is the cost of failure in the supply chain so high for the aerospace industry?

Control of the supply chain turns critical

by Stephen Pritchard

A An efficient supply chain is a prize worth working for. According to the consultancy firm Accenture, 'supply chain leadership' can increase a
5 company's market value by between 7 and 26 per cent above the industry average. But for a business, even competing for that prize demands a significant investment in resources. In
10 sectors such as consumer goods and retailing, established companies have already achieved the easiest supply-chain efficiencies. Making further improvements is much more difficult.

B Nonetheless, an efficient supply chain is a must for a widening range of businesses. Fashion, hi-tech and grocery retailers realised early on the importance of ensuring the right stock
20 reached the right store at the right time. No one wants a warehouse full of summer dresses at the beginning of autumn, or indeed shelves of last season's mobile phones in the weeks before
25 Christmas. But the supply chain is now moving up the agenda in slower-moving sectors, such as heavy manufacturing.

C Effective supply-chain management is the only way to make efficient
30 use of global sourcing strategies, and especially the huge manufacturing capacity of China and south-east Asia. Although globalisation has reduced production costs in a wide range of
35 sectors, the trend to source components or even finished goods from China and elsewhere has made the supply-chain manager's task far harder. 'Our internal systems handle more than 700
40 suppliers,' says Christian Verstraete, worldwide supply-chain expert at Hewlett-Packard. 'We have to be able to exchange messages not just with them, but with their suppliers.'

D Supply-chain managers in many sectors are looking for greater visibility of what is happening in their supply chains and faster access to more accurate data. This means that if there is an
50 unexpected event, such as storms affecting shipping or a production shortfall, companies can divert stocks or bring in alternative suppliers. 'Companies are not just asking suppliers
55 why there is a problem with an order,' says Sanjiv Sidu, President of i2, a vendor of management software for supply chains. 'They are asking: "When did you first know, and why
60 did you surprise me?"'

E In sectors such as retail, supply-chain problems lead to 'stock-outs' or empty shelves, which send customers elsewhere. In heavy or complex manufac-
65 turing, supply-chain problems can lead to cancelled orders running into billions of dollars, or severe penalties for late delivery.

F As manufacturers move away from
70 vertically integrated production, where all steps of the production process are controlled in-house, the supply chain suddenly becomes critical. 'In aerospace and defence, we are 10 years
75 behind the hi-tech or even automotive sectors, and how we improve the performance of our supply chain is quite a challenge,' explains Bill Black, Chief Quality Officer at aerospace manufac-
80 turer EADS. 'The cost of running our supply-chain logistics is minor, set against the $100m cost of an aircraft. But the cost of failure is enormous.'

G 'About 80 per cent of the cost of an
85 aircraft is accounted for by suppliers and partners,' says Black, making EADS 'a co-ordinator of complex products'. 'I need to know if an event can affect our master schedule, and that
90 means that I need to know what is happening, not just with my tier-one suppliers, but with tier-three, -four or -five suppliers as well.'

FT

VOCABULARY

A Word search

Find words or phrases in the article which fit these meanings.

1 companies which sell products to the public (paragraph B)
2 goods or products which are stored and waiting to be sold (paragraph B)
3 another name for a shop (paragraph B)
4 a place to store goods (paragraph B)
5 to buy or get materials, components, etc. (paragraph C)
6 when not enough goods are produced by a manufacturer (paragraph D)
7 send to a different destination (paragraph D)
8 a company that sells to another company (paragraph D)
9 when shops have empty shelves (paragraph E)
10 financial punishments (paragraph E)
11 direct suppliers to a customer (paragraph G)
12 suppliers to the suppliers of a company's direct suppliers, suppliers to those suppliers, etc. (paragraph G)

B Words often confused

1 Look at the use of *efficient* and *effective* in this sentence and choose the best definition (a or b) for each word.

*Effective supply-chain management is the only way to make **efficient** use of global sourcing strategies.*

a) when something works well, especially in terms of time and costs
b) when something works well and produces a good result

2 Complete these sentences with either *efficient* or *effective*.

1 To remain competitive, companies need to have highly .... supply chains.
2 Companies that manage their core processes in a more cost-........ way than their competitors will gain the advantage in the marketplace.
3 Suppliers and customers need to have .... communication systems in order to share information about production needs.
4 A well-run supply chain can make a company more ...., leading to significantly reduced production costs.

C Word partnerships

Match these words to make noun–noun partnerships from the article.

1 production   a) value
2 manufacturing   b) goods
3 market   c) capacity
4 industry   d) costs
5 production   e) average
6 consumer   f) shortfall

D Verbs and prepositions

Complete these sentences using the prepositions in the box.

against	away	for	for	for	for	from	in	into	to	up

1 An efficient supply chain is a prize worth working . . . .

2 It needs a lot of resources to compete . . . . the prize of an efficient supply chain.

3 The importance of the supply chain is moving . . . . the agenda.

4 Supply-chain managers are looking . . . . faster access to information.

5 In cases of production shortfalls, companies may need to bring . . . . alternative suppliers.

6 In the retail sector, supply-chain problems can lead . . . . empty shelves.

7 The cost of cancelled orders can run . . . . billions of dollars.

8 Manufacturers are moving . . . . vertically integrated production.

9 The costs of running supply chains in the aerospace industry are small when set . . . . the cost of building an aircraft.

10 About 80 per cent of the cost of an aircraft is accounted . . . . by suppliers and partners.

E Vocabulary development

Match these words and phrases (a–j) with the verbs + prepositions in Exercise D that they can replace (1–10).

a) result in

b) taken up

c) trying hard to get

d) use / work with

e) leaving / changing from

f) try to win

g) compared with

h) want

i) amount to

j) becoming more important on

OVER TO YOU

1 Based on the information in the article and your own experience, explain why an efficient supply chain is essential for all kinds of businesses. Give examples.

2 Why is effective supply-chain management so important for European companies which source components from China and other parts of Asia?

3 Why does the supply chain become critical when manufacturers move away from vertically integrated production?

4 The main reason for a global sourcing strategy is cost reduction. What are some of the hidden costs of this strategy?

Using the supply chain to increase sales

This unit describes how Procter & Gamble is using its supply chain not only to improve profits but also to increase sales growth.

Discuss these questions.

1 In what ways do you think a company producing consumer products can use its supply chain to increase sales growth?
2 What are the benefits to retailers if their suppliers have efficient supply chains?
3 How can deliveries to the distribution centre of a retailer be made more efficient?

A Understanding the main points

Read the article on the opposite page and choose the statement that expresses the ideas in the article most accurately.

1 Suppliers need to reduce their supply-chain costs because of increased transport costs.
2 By reducing supply-chain costs, Procter & Gamble (P&G) is achieving higher profits.
3 P&G is using its supply chain to increase sales growth.

B Understanding details

Read the article again and answer these questions.

1 What is Keith Harrison's job, and when did he start it?
2 How big is P&G's supply chain?
3 What pressure are retailers and suppliers under?
4 What is one thing that P&G is trying to do with its supply chain?
5 What else is P&G trying to do with its supply chain?
6 How does supply-chain management usually operate in a company?
7 How can a supplier's effective supply chain help retailers?
8 What does P&G want from its customers if it improves its supply-chain performance and reduces their out-of-stocks and inventory levels?
9 How important a customer is Wal-Mart for P&G?
10 What kind of co-operation do Wal-Mart and P&G have?
11 Is P&G the only company to have access to Wal-Mart's Retail Link data?
12 What is special about P&G's Missouri factory?

Adding value with the supply chain

by Jonathan Birchall

A As the manager in charge of the world's largest supply chain, Keith Harrison believes the time has come to give the business of logistics more credit.
5 The Head of Global Product Supply at Procter & Gamble believes the search for a competitive edge will focus more on supply-chain efficiency as retailers and suppliers battle huge increases
10 in raw material and energy costs. 'Today you have road congestion, you have freight costs, driver shortages, capacity issues. Working capital is at a premium. Competition among
15 retailers and vendors is higher. All of this is putting pressure on having a more efficient supply chain. This is more critical than it has been before.'

B Since his appointment in 2001,
20 Mr Harrison has been at the forefront of efforts to drive costs from P&G's supply chain, helping the company meet its long-term sales and earnings growth targets, in spite of surging
25 input costs. But he says P&G has also been looking increasingly over the past three years at ways to turn improvements in the supply chain into top-line sales growth. 'We're trying to make the
30 supply chain into a growth engine for the company,' he says. 'A lot of the time, supply-chain management is reactive, or passive, cost control. But we think there's also an opportunity for
35 us also to use the supply chain to create top-line growth as well as bottom-line performance.'

C An effective supply chain helps manufacturers by reducing a retailer's
40 'out-of-stocks', which in turn prevents lost sales. Those sales also benefit the retailer, while efficient delivery of products to meet demand can also reduce the costs of holding inventory
45 to the retailer.

D P&G is telling retailers that it should be rewarded for the benefits its supply chain delivers. 'If I do something with my supply chain to reduce my
50 customer's inventories, I want more than just the "supplier of the year" award,' he says. 'How do we get that value that we've created at least partially reinvested in growing our
55 business? Do we get sharper pricing, better features, more display, better shelving?'

E As an example of the potential benefits, Mr Harrison gives the example
60 of a pilot project with Wal-Mart in the US, whose worldwide stores account for 15 per cent of P&G's overall sales. The two established a cooperative relationship in the late 1980s, starting
65 with Wal-Mart's decision to allow P&G and other suppliers access to the customer sales data collected by its Retail Link computer system.

F Over the past 12 months, a P&G
70 factory in Missouri has been using live sales data from stores not to forecast demand but to schedule replenishment deliveries on a store-by-store basis for a single test product. Rather than
75 shipping the required volume to a distribution centre, where it is then divided up for each store, the shipments are instead prepared at the factory for the right store. When the goods arrive at
80 the Wal-Mart distribution centre, they are moved directly from P&G's truck to the appropriate Wal-Mart truck, with no time in storage. 'It is assembled for a store, and it is just flowing through
85 the system,' says Mr Harrison.

G Kevin O'Marah, a logistics consultant at AMR Research, believes P&G is the first consumer goods company to use the Retail Link data in this way.

FT

VOCABULARY

A Word search

Find words or phrases in the article which fit these meanings.

1 something that gives a company an advantage over others (paragraph A)
2 fight against (paragraph A)
3 extremely valuable and rare, which a lot of people want (paragraph A)
4 in the leading position (paragraph B)
5 rapidly increasing (paragraph B)
6 the way goods are arranged in a store so they are easily seen by customers (paragraph D)
7 a test done on a small scale to see how something works (paragraph E)
8 information about sales, which is current or in real time (paragraph F)
9 replacement of what has been used or sold (paragraph F)
10 put together in a certain way (paragraph F)

B Sentence completion

Use the words and phrases in the box to complete the sentences.

> cost control   freight costs   growth targets   inventory   replenishment deliveries
> road congestion   sales data   vendors   working capital

1 To keep costs down, it is important for retailers to keep their .... levels as low as possible.
2 If retailers carry too much stock, they will use a lot of their ....
3 A more cost-effective way to operate is to schedule .... on a just-in-time basis.
4 If suppliers have live access to a customer's ...., they can prepare deliveries specially for each store.
5 Suppliers are also known as ....
6 Delivering goods by truck now takes longer in many countries due to increased ....
7 With rising oil prices, ... are also going up.
8 A traditional aim of supply-chain managers is ...., keeping costs down.
9 P&G is using its supply chain to meet sales ....

C Word families

Complete the chart.

noun	verb	noun	verb
shipment	 1	investment	 6
distribution	 2	replenishment	 7
growth	 3	storage	 8
improvement	 4	competition	 9
delivery	 5	manufacturer	 10

D Understanding expressions

Choose the best explanation for each phrase from the article.

1 '... *capacity issues*.' (line 13)
   a) problems about the company's expertise
   b) problems about production volumes

2 '... *input costs*.' (line 25)
   a) costs of materials purchased by a company
   b) costs of manpower employed by a company

3 '... *top-line sales growth*.' (lines 28–29)
   a) increased sales turnover
   b) better sales of the most profitable products

4 '... *a growth engine* for the company ...' (line 30–31)
   a) something that will make the company bigger
   b) something that will help the company increase sales

5 '... *bottom-line performance*.' (lines 36–37)
   a) better sales of poor performing products
   b) better profitability

6 '... *sharper pricing* ...' (line 55)
   a) more competitive prices
   b) more risky prices

E Describing a process

We often use the passive form of the verb to describe a process.

Put the verbs in brackets into the correct form of the passive.

Rather than shipping the required volume to a distribution centre, where it .... then ....[1] (divide) up for each store, the shipments .... instead ....[2] (prepare) at the factory for individual stores. So, when the goods arrive at the Wal-Mart distribution centre, they ....[3] (move) directly from P&G's truck to the appropriate Wal-Mart truck, with no time in storage. It ....[4] (assemble) for a store, and it is just flowing through the system.

OVER TO YOU

1 Imagine you are the supply-chain manager at a consumer goods manufacturer like P&G. Hold a meeting with your customer, a large supermarket chain. Argue for things such as sharper pricing and better display of your products in return for reducing the customer's costs of holding inventory levels because of the efficiency of your supply chain.

2 Give a presentation to the board of your company to explain how using your customers' live sales data can help reduce their inventory levels and at the same time increase sales of your company's products.

The global supply chain

This unit describes how Nike, the US sports shoe producer, operates its global supply chain.

BEFORE YOU READ

Discuss these questions.

1 When you hear the name 'Nike', what images come to your mind?
2 How much of Nike's sports shoe production do you think is based in the US?
3 What do you understand by the term *virtual enterprise*?

READING

A Understanding the main points

Read the article on the opposite page and answer these questions.

1 What is the profile of Nike products in the marketplace?
2 How much of Nike's shoe production is outsourced?
3 How important is product innovation for Nike?
4 How does Nike co-ordinate its complex global production and distribution activities?

B Understanding details

Read the article again and say whether these statements are true (T), false (F) or there is not enough information given (N). Identify the part of the article that gives this information.

1 Nike sports shoes are mass-market products.
2 Running an efficient supply chain is a key to Nike's success.
3 Nike has a very small number of full-time employees.
4 Nike outsources most of its R&D.
5 Nike designs its basketball shoe in the US.
6 Nike's basketball shoes are the only product manufactured in the US.
7 All of Nike's products go through at least 120 checks before they are released onto the market.
8 Nike releases more than 300 new shoe designs each year.
9 Nike sometimes gets its sales forecasts wrong and is left with unsold stock.
10 Nike outsources the distribution of finished products in the US and Europe.
11 Nike is planning to move away from sports shoes and into sports equipment, clothing, watches and eyewear.

The logistics challenge of global business

A In little more than a generation, US-based sports company Nike Inc. reinvented the concept of the sports shoe. It transformed the cheapest of mass-market footwear into high-tech, high-performance products, with all the cachet of haute
5 couture and carrying price tags to match.

B Technologically, Nike's products are leading edge, as is its brand-led marketing, which successfully used sporting-superstar endorsement to establish the brand as an icon of youth subculture. However, as in any global organisation,
10 logistics and the management of the supply chain is a crucial strategic issue at Nike.

C From its headquarters in Beaverton, Oregon, Nike operates a globe-spanning virtual enterprise. At its core are a set of business processes, designed to combine its
15 state-of-the-art R&D capabilities with a ruthlessly low-cost manufacturing strategy. The company outsources virtually 100 per cent of its shoe production, for example, retaining in-house manufacturing of a few key components of its patented Nike Air System.

D Nike's basketball shoe, for example, is designed in Oregon and Tennessee and developed jointly by Asian and US technicians in Oregon, Taiwan and South Korea. The shoes themselves are manufactured in South Korea (men's sizes) and in Indonesia (boy's sizes), from 72 components
25 supplied by companies in Japan, South Korea, Taiwan, Indonesia and the United States. Moreover, the complexity of the product means that it passes through more than 120 pairs of hands during the production process. It also means that there is a danger of extended lead times.

E Tying the whole Nike enterprise together are information systems that co-ordinate each step of these far-flung activities, and a logistics infrastructure capable of bringing the components together at precisely the right time, as well as managing the supply of finished goods into the
35 global marketplace.

F Significantly, both are flexible enough to cope with the constant product, materials and process innovation, allowing the company to bring more than 300 new shoe designs to market each year. However, this punishing rate of innova-
40 tion brings with it high levels of finished inventory if sales forecasts are not achieved.

G In the United States and Europe, primary distribution of Nike products is increasingly outsourced to specialist third parties, who are linked into the company's global-sales and
45 customer-service support systems. These links allow the contractors to prioritise shipments and manage order fulfilment as cost effectively as possible, while ensuring that product-availability information is readily accessible to all decision-makers throughout Nike's virtual enterprise.

H Importantly, too, these organisational capabilities will be extremely useful for Nike if fashion-conscious young consumers turn away from designer sports shoes, forcing the company to rely more heavily on sales of its widening portfolio of sports equipment, clothing, watches
55 and eyewear.

I When the supply chains are global and the products are fashion oriented, the management of logistics becomes a key factor in business success or failure.

from *Logistics and Supply Chain Management –
Creating Value-Adding Networks* by Martin Christopher

VOCABULARY

A Understanding expressions

Choose the best explanation for each word or phrase from the article.

1 '... with all the *cachet* of haute couture ...' (lines 4–5)
   a) special reputation
   b) style

2 '... and *carrying price tags to match*.' (line 5)
   a) with prices similar to other sports shoes
   b) with prices similar to other high-fashion items

3 '... as *an icon of youth subculture*.' (lines 8–9)
   a) something both famous and fashionable to young people
   b) a symbol of youthful rebellion

4 '... Nike operates *a globe-spanning virtual enterprise*.' (lines 12–13)
   a) Nike has subsidiaries and plants in many parts of the world.
   b) Nike produces and sells worldwide, but does not have employees in lots of countries.

5 '... with *a ruthlessly low-cost manufacturing strategy*.' (lines 15–16)
   a) Nike treats its production workers very poorly.
   b) Nike is very strict about keeping production costs down.

6 '... there is *a danger of extended lead times*.' (line 29)
   a) It is possible that Nike products may sometimes come onto the market ahead of schedule.
   b) It is possible that Nike products may sometimes be late to market.

7 '*Tying the whole Nike enterprise together* are information systems ...' (lines 30–31)
   a) coordinating everything the company does
   b) making the process too complicated

8 '... this *punishing* rate of innovation ...' (lines 39–40)
   a) unusually high
   b) dangerously high

B Word partnerships

Match these words to make noun–noun partnerships from the article.

1	information	a)	availability
2	business	b)	times
3	manufacturing	c)	forecasts
4	production	d)	infrastructure
5	lead	e)	processes
6	logistics	f)	service
7	sales	g)	process
8	customer	h)	strategy
9	order	i)	systems
10	product	j)	fulfilment

C **Sentence completion**

Use the word partnerships from Exercise B to complete these sentences.

1 A complex supply chain spread over different parts of the world can sometimes result in long ....

2 Nike's .... enable it to co-ordinate all the steps in its complex virtual enterprise.

3 Nike has highly developed .... to ensure that it can coordinate all aspects of its supply chain as effectively as possible.

4 Nike baseball shoes go through a very complex ....

5 If Nike gets its .... wrong, it can be left with a lot of unsold stock at its retail outlets.

6 In the US and Europe, delivery and .... for customers are outsourced to contractors.

7 Nike's .... enables components from different parts of the world to be brought together in the right place at the right time.

8 To keep its production costs down, Nike has a very low-cost ....

9 Making sure customers get what they need and are satisfied is the role of the .... department.

10 In order to be able to replenish stocks quickly, the distributors need to have up-to-the-minute information about ....

D **Word search**

There are a lot of word partnerships in the article which function as adjectives. All of them have a hyphen, e.g. *high-tech* (paragraph A).

Find adjectival word partnerships in the article which fit these meanings.

1 located in the US (paragraph A)

2 selling in high volumes at low prices (paragraph A)

3 with a very good performance (paragraph A)

4 where the product name and image is most important (paragraph B)

5 in all parts of the world (paragraph C)

6 extremely up to date (paragraph C)

7 spending as little money as possible (paragraph C)

8 internally in the company (paragraph C)

9 in distant locations (paragraph E)

10 strongly influenced by trends in fashion (paragraph H)

OVER TO YOU

1 Nike outsources almost all of its shoe production, as well as its distribution in Europe and the US. In fact, it is called a *globe-spanning virtual enterprise*. What are the pros and cons of Nike's business strategy?

2 Nike has had some bad publicity in recent years about the working conditions in some of the factories in developing countries where its shoes are manufactured. Given the outsourcing business model Nike uses, how can the company ensure that its suppliers comply with good employment practice?

The importance of good supplier relationships

This unit looks at the importance of choosing good suppliers for an efficient supply chain.

BEFORE YOU READ

Discuss these questions.

1   In your view, what are the three most frequent causes of difficulties in supply chains?

2   Do you think it is better to manage the sourcing of components and materials internally (in house) or through external suppliers? Is it the same for all types of products and materials?

3   Many companies use 'just-in-time management', a system which has material and parts arriving just before they are needed.
   a)   Why has it become so popular?
   b)   What are the risks for the supply chain?
   c)   What can be done to minimise them?

READING

A   **Understanding the main points**

Read the article on the opposite page and answer these questions.

1   What action did Apple take that caused such a lot of disagreement in the computer world?

2   According to the writer, what are the three most frequent sources of problems in the supply chain?

3   What two trends have made it even more important for companies to avoid delays with supplies?

4   In order to produce high-quality products, what must companies look for in their suppliers?

5   The writer mentions two strategies that companies can choose for sourcing materials and components. What are they?

6   When companies source components through supplier companies, what should they do to increase the chances of success?

B   **Understanding details**

Read paragraphs D–G of the article again and answer these questions.

1   What are the potential consequences for companies when there are short delays in the supply of critical components?

2   According to the writer, what are the potential benefits for a company that can respond to customer needs faster than its competitors?

3   What are the consequences for companies that fail to source good-quality components and have them delivered on time?

4   According to Hakan Hakansson, what three qualities are important for making partnerships between companies and their suppliers work?

An alliance that can supply a competitive edge

by **Morgen Witzel**

A In 2005, Apple Computers announced an end to its relationship with IBM as supplier of microprocessors for its desktop computers. The naming of Intel, the world's biggest semi conductor company, as its replacement caused controversy within the industry. How well would Apple manage the transition to the new supplier, a process that could take anything up to two years? Would the company be able to achieve the benefits it expected from the new relationship? Most observers were confident that the answer would be yes to both questions, but the move also had serious risks.

B The developments at Apple are a sharp reminder of the importance of good suppliers, and developing strong relationships with them, in order to ensure continuity and consistency of supply. When supply chains fail to work efficiently, the entire business faces problems.

C Difficulties with the supply chain typically relate to three issues: cost, quality and timeliness. The first issue is critical: companies organise their supply chains in order to reduce the costs of materials and components as far as possible. But the others – timeliness and quality – can also be extremely important.

D Given the widespread use of just-in-time management in industrial production, even short delays in the supply of critical components can cause knock-on delays in the production process, in turn reducing profits. Time is also important to customers. Increasingly, they demand that companies respond faster to their needs. Companies that can respond more quickly than the industry average can expect to be twice as profitable as their competitors. They can also expect to grow up to three times more quickly. Obviously, none of this can happen if the company's own suppliers are not equally timely.

E As for quality, good products can be created only from good materials and components, so choosing suppliers who are committed to high quality is vital. If companies cannot source good-quality components and have them delivered on time, their own products will be late to market and have defects. When this happens, any advantage in terms of price will quickly disappear.

F In order to establish control in all three areas, managers have two main options for managing the supply process. The first is to manage as much of it as possible in house or through wholly owned subsidiaries. The second is to source components and materials through the market, using supplier companies.

G Buying components and materials from independent suppliers has become the preferred solution for many companies. But for this to work, it is necessary to build strong partnerships with suppliers. According to Hakan Hakansson, professor at Sweden's University of Uppsala, the most important element in any supply-chain relationship is commitment among those involved. Suppliers and customers must be open with each other and trust each other for the system to function efficiently.

FT

VOCABULARY

A   Definitions

Match these words and phrases from the article (1–10) with their meanings (a–j).

1	controversy	a)	relationships between companies who work together
2	transition	b)	faults or imperfections
3	continuity	c)	happening at exactly the right time
4	consistency	d)	strong belief and willingness to do something
5	timeliness	e)	continuing over time without interrupts or problems
6	knock-on delays	f)	always being of the same standard
7	defects	g)	a strong disagreement
8	subsidiary	h)	a change from one situation to another
9	partnerships	i)	a company owned by a larger company
10	commitment	j)	when a delay causes several other delays, one after the other

B   Word search

1   Find words or phrases in the article with a similar meaning.

   1   whole (paragraph B)
   2   are connected with (paragraph C)
   3   very important (paragraph C)
   4   extensive (paragraph D)
   5   react (paragraph D)
   6   obtain (paragraph E)
   7   owned completely (paragraph F)
   8   honest and not secretive (paragraph G)
   9   work (paragraph G)

2   Find two expressions in Exercise A that are used to talk about timing.

3   Find three other expressions in paragraphs D and E of the article that refer to timing.

4   Think of at least two other words or phrases you can use to describe a delivery that was late.

C   Text completion

Use words and phrases from Exercise B to complete this description.

Because our main supplier failed to deliver o........t........ [1], there were serious k........-o........d........ [2] at each stage of the manufacturing process. The result was that the new Rimo X9 was l........t........m........ [3]. In company like ours, t........ [4] is of critical importance, so we must take action. Unless they can guarantee more t........ [5] deliveries in future, we will need to find an alternative supplier.

D Word partnerships

Match the adjectives (1–8) with the nouns (a–h) to make expressions from the article.

1	serious	a)	subsidiary
2	strong	b)	delays
3	entire	c)	relationships/partnerships
4	widespread	d)	quality
5	short/knock-on	e)	business
6	critical/good-quality	f)	use
7	high	g)	risks
8	wholly owned	h)	components

E Sentence completion

Complete these sentences using verbs from the box in the correct form.

> build   cause   have   respond   source

1   Late deliveries of materials and components can .... knock-on delays at each stage of the production process.

2   Companies will be more profitable if they are able to .... to customer needs quickly.

3   Companies that only .... components and materials from one supplier are putting themselves at risk.

4   .... good relationships with your suppliers is critical for ensuring consistent supplies.

5   Nearly 25 per cent of the products in the last delivery .... defects.

F Vocabulary development

1   Find two more phrases in this extract from the article which are used to make comparisons.

*Companies that can respond **more** quickly **than** the industry average can expect to be twice as profitable as their competitors. They can also expect to grow up to three times more quickly.*

2   Use similar phrases to write your own sentences making the case for just-in-time manufacturing.

- -er / more ... than
- twice / three/four times as ... as
- three/four times more ...

OVER TO YOU

1   What are the benefits and risks of sourcing materials and components through a network of suppliers? What steps can be taken to minimise the risks? Write a short report summarising your views.

2   What practical steps can a company take to build strong relationships with its suppliers?

3   Write an e-mail to a supply company. You have noticed a small increase in the number of defects in its last two orders. You are also concerned that the last order was late and are worried about the potential impact it could have on your ability to meet orders if this continues.

Minimising risks with suppliers

This unit suggests ways companies can minimise the risk to their business when suppliers get into financial difficulties.

BEFORE YOU READ

Discuss these questions.

1 What are the early warning signs that a supplier is in difficulties, e.g. late deliveries, attempts to change payment terms?

2 What are the risks for a company and its supply chain if a main supplier gets into financial difficulties?

3 What can companies do to detect as early as possible if a supplier is in trouble?

READING

A Understanding the main points

1 Read the article on the opposite page and say whether these statements are true (T) or false (F). Correct the false ones.

1 Edscha is a key supplier for BMW.

2 Edscha is no longer in business.

3 The problem of failures among suppliers mostly affects the car sector.

2 The article includes five proposals for minimising the risk of supplier problems. Mark the order in which the writer mentions them.

a) Extend ratings and communication to your suppliers' suppliers.

b) Put in place an early warning system to alert you to potential problems.

c) Check the interconnections between your suppliers, for example if they use the same suppliers or supply the same industry or companies.

d) Set up a rating system to analyse suppliers' financial performance.

e) Communicate regularly and build strong relationships with suppliers.

B Understanding details

Read the article again and answer these questions.

1 Why did BMW decide to support Edscha when it got into financial difficulty?

2 What action has BMW taken in response to the crisis with Edscha to protect its supply chain from disruption?

3 What two steps has it taken to check the financial health of critical suppliers?

4 What example does Stephen Wagner give to illustrate the importance of extending ratings to its supplier's suppliers?

Early warnings in the supply chain

by Richard Milne

A When Edscha, a German manufacturer of sun roofs and other car parts, filed for insolvency early in 2009, it presented BMW with a crisis. The luxury carmaker was about to introduce a new model – and Edscha supplied its roof. 'We had no option of going to another supplier, as that would have taken six months and we don't have that time. We had to help Edscha survive,' BMW says.

B Today, Edscha is still in business, because of the support offered by its leading clients, including BMW. However, BMW is still so worried about disruption to its supply chain that it has increased the number of staff in its risk-monitoring department with responsibility for component makers.

C Such concerns are felt not just in the German automotive industry. Failures among important suppliers affect many sectors, from manufacturing to retail. So how should companies monitor whether their suppliers are getting into difficulty? And what should they do if they get into trouble?

D It is essential to maintain good relationships with suppliers. Stephan Wagner, a professor in logistics management in Germany, says one of the simplest solutions is to communicate: 'Talk to them. That will give you a very good feel for what is going on.'

E The Swiss Federal Institute of Technology (ETH) in Zurich proposes four steps, some already widely used but others followed by only a few.

F The first step recommended by ETH is to establish a rating system for a company's primary suppliers. The ratings should be based on financial information, with cashflow more important in many cases than profitability. BMW looks at a variety of issues, including the ownership structure. It also maintains close contact with Audi and Mercedes, its main competitors, to swap information on suppliers.

G The second, related, proposal is to set up an early warning system that monitors what is happening in the present. Such a system looks at operational issues such as whether quality problems are increasing at a particular supplier, as well as financial issues, such as any attempt to change payment terms.

H The third recommendation is to extend the ratings and communication with suppliers further down the chain. Professor Wagner says: 'Many companies don't even know who their second-tier suppliers are.' He points to the example of a German carmaker where production nearly stopped after the sub-supplier of material for its seats went bankrupt.

I The final proposal is to examine the interdependencies in a company's supply base. According to Professor Wagner, many companies with dual or multiple sourcing are confident that they would be able to switch supplier if one got into trouble. But research by ETH suggests this confidence may be misplaced: if one supplier in a particular area goes bankrupt, the probability increases that other suppliers in that sector will become insolvent.

VOCABULARY

A Definitions

1 Find words or phrases in the article which match these meanings.

   1 a situation when a company is unable to pay what it owes its creditors (paragraph A)

   2 a time of great danger or difficulty (paragraph A)

   3 interruption of normal activity (paragraph B)

   4 the name of a department responsible for checking the status of risks (paragraph B)

   5 when businesses have to close because of lack of success (paragraph C)

   6 watch and check over a period time to see how something is progressing (paragraph C)

   7 a systematic method of evaluating how good suppliers are (paragraph F)

   8 a series of steps for spotting potential problems with suppliers (paragraph G)

   9 ways in which organisations are dependent on each other (paragraph I)

   10 formally declares it is unable to pay its creditors (paragraph I)

2 Which of the words or phrases in Exercise 1 are used to describe:

   a) risk management?   b) company failure?

B Word families

Complete the chart with words from the article used to describe failure in companies.

noun	adjectives	verb / verb–noun phrase
........¹	failed	to fail
........²	........³	to ....⁴ insolvency (= to ask formally) to ....⁵ insolvent
bankruptcy	........⁶	to go into bankruptcy to ....⁷ bankrupt / to be declared bankrupt

C Definitions

1 Match these words and phrases from the article (1–5) with their meanings (a–e).

   1 primary supplier   a) using two suppliers for the same component or service

   2 second-tier supplier   b) using many suppliers for the same component or service

   3 dual sourcing   c) all the suppliers a company works with

   4 multiple sourcing   d) a company that supplies components or services direct to the final customer, also called a tier-one supplier

   5 supplier base   e) a company that supplies components and services to a primary/tier-one supplier

2 What do you think the phrase *single sourcing* means in this sentence?

*For its fan assemblies, Computer Ace has adopted **single sourcing** and finds that working closely with this one partner ensures consistent quality.*

D   **Sentence completion**

Use the phrases from Exercise C to complete these sentences.

1 In a radical restructuring of its supply chain, V-ray Enterprises has cut its .... by 20 per cent and plans to lose more suppliers next year.

2 As part of its risk-management strategy, V-ray has set up a team that will support its four .... suppliers and also make regular visits to its ....-........ suppliers.

3 A well-known Japanese electronics company now uses two suppliers for each of its main components. It believes this move to .... will protect it from supply disruption.

4 .... worked for Arc Technology because it encouraged competition between suppliers, which helped to keep prices down.

5 One advantage of .... is that it allows a company to build a strong, mutually beneficial relationship with its supplier.

E   **Word search**

Find words or phrases in the article which can replace the expressions in italic in these guidelines for managing supplier risk.

1 Watch for signs that a supplier is *starting to have problems*, for example late deliveries or requests to change payment terms.

2 *Establish* early warning and rating systems.

3 *Carefully watch and check* what is going on at your suppliers.

4 Try to *keep* good relationships with your suppliers.

5 It essential to *talk to* suppliers to find out exactly is going on.

6 Where possible, *exchange* information about suppliers with your main competitors.

7 *Spread* your rating system to suppliers further down the supply chain.

8 If one of your suppliers is in difficulties, it may be possible to *change* to another supplier.

9 Act early; don't wait until your supplier is about to *go out of business*.

OVER TO YOU

1 Discuss the advantages and risks of a) single sourcing, b) dual sourcing, and c) multiple sourcing key components and services for a minimum of three different types of products.
   Present your sourcing strategy for each of your chosen products, highlighting the benefits.

2 Research a company which has tried to help a supplier out of difficulties. What action did it take? Was it a failure or a success? What lessons could other companies learn from this case?

3 Design a checklist that could be used to monitor the operational and financial health of your suppliers.

Managing unexpected events and disasters

This unit looks at how two companies responded to a natural disaster at a supplier factory and handled the risk to their supplies.

Discuss these questions.

1   Think of three unexpected events or natural disasters that can cause major disruption to supply chains, e.g. a fire, serious storm, a strike. What are the potential consequences for companies of each chosen event?

2   How possible is it for companies to plan for disasters like these?

3   What can they do to minimise the impact and get the supply chain back to normal?

A   **Understanding the main points**

Read the article on the opposite page and choose the best option to complete each statement.

1   The fire took place at *Philips Electronics' / Nokia's* plant in New Mexico.

2   It destroyed all supplies of *mobile phones / silicon chips* in the plant.

3   Nokia and Ericsson were informed about the fire and probable delays to their supplies *the day it happened / three days later*.

4   *Nokia / Ericsson* was first to detect a problem with its supplies from Philips Electronics.

5   As a result of the fire, production of chips was stopped for *about a week / several months*.

6   *Nokia / Ericsson* was able to find alternative supplies to meet its orders.

7   The effects of the fire and disruption to supplies were most serious for *Nokia / Ericsson*.

8   *Nokia / Ericsson* was most effective in dealing with the crisis caused by the fire.

B   **Understanding details**

Read the article again and answer these questions.

1   What first made Nokia suspect there might be problem with supplies from Philips?

2   What action did Nokia take after it found out about the fire and probable delays in supplying chips?

3   When Nokia realised how serious the problem was, what two steps did it take to make sure it had supplies of chips to meet its orders?

4   What were the short- and long-term effects of the fire and halt in production for:

a) Ericsson?

b) Nokia?

Two responses to a potential disaster

A In 2000, worldwide demand for mobile phones was booming, and shortages of critical components were a regular threat to growth. Two of the global leaders were the Finnish electronics company Nokia and its Swedish
5 competitor Ericsson.

B On 17 March 2000, lightning caused a fire in Philips Electronics' silicon-chip manufacturing plant in New Mexico. The fire was under control in minutes, but not before it destroyed silicon chips for thousands of mobile
10 phones. Even worse, damage from the smoke and water contaminated the complete stock of millions of chips, ready for shipment.

C Philips reacted immediately, giving priority to its customers according to the value of their business. Together,
15 Nokia and its competitor Ericsson accounted for 40% of its production. Philips therefore made a decision to meet their orders first once the plant returned to normal. However, it did not inform them about the fire until three days later.

D Within two days, Nokia's computer systems detected that
20 shipments of some Philips' chips seemed delayed. On 20 March, a components purchasing manager called Philips about the problem and was informed about the fire and probable disruption to production for around a week.

E As a matter of routine, Nokia put the five components
25 produced at the Philips plant on a special monitoring list. They began checking the status of these five components once a day instead of the usual once a week.

F By the end of March, it was clear to both Nokia and Philips that the problem was so serious that supplies would
30 be disrupted for several months. Aware that this could affect the production of several million mobile phones, Nokia decided to take steps to secure supplies.

G Executives at Nokia put pressure on Philips to work with them to develop alternative plans to maintain supplies.
35 Philips responded by asking their other plants to use any additional capacity to meet Nokia's needs.

H In addition, Nokia sent a team to its other chip suppliers in the US and Japan to negotiate priority status for supplies of chips and to persuade them to ramp up production. Two
40 of them responded within five days, agreeing to lead times of less than a week.

I Ericsson remained unaware of the potential disruption to their orders until three days after the fire when Philips called. They believed Philips' explanation that the fire was only
45 a minor event, so did not take action until early April. By then, Nokia had already secured supplies. Unlike Nokia, Ericsson had no alternative sources of supply. It had decided earlier to single-source key components as a way of simplifying its supply chain.

J Ericsson lost an estimated $400m in sales as a result of the fire, and was finally forced to stop manufacturing mobile phones. In contrast, Nokia was able to maintain production levels throughout the event and strengthen its position as European market leader.

from *Logistics and Supply Chain Management – Creating Value-Adding Networks* by Martin Christopher

VOCABULARY

A Definitions

Match these words and phrases from the article (1–10) with their meanings (a–j).

1	shortages	a)	a factory where an industrial process takes place
2	threat	b)	the ability to produce a larger amount
3	plant	c)	damaged so badly it cannot be used
4	destroyed	d)	the transportation of goods
5	contaminated	e)	high importance in relation to others
6	shipment	f)	not enough of something
7	priority	g)	time between receiving an order and delivering it
8	disruption	h)	made unusable by contact with something harmful
9	capacity	i)	a source of danger
10	lead time	j)	when a problem interrupts something and prevents it from continuing

B Word search

1 Find words or phrases in the article which have similar meanings.

1 increasing and successful (paragraph A)
2 represented (paragraph C)
3 to obtain something you need (paragraph F)
4 to increase (paragraph H)
5 small and not serious (paragraph I)
6 making less complicated (paragraph I)
7 approximately calculated (paragraph J)
8 make stronger (paragraph J)

2 In paragraph E, find the expression that tells you it is the usual procedure for Nokia to monitor components when they detect a possible problem.

3 The word *status* is used in lines 26 and 38, but has different meanings.
Match each use with its meaning (a or b).

a) position in relation to others
b) situation at a given time

C Word partnerships

Match the verbs (1–6) with the nouns (a–f).

1	secure	a)	production
2	take	b)	supplies
3	ramp up	c)	steps/action
4	single-source	d)	production levels
5	maintain	e)	priority status
6	negotiate	f)	components

D Prepositions

1 Complete these sentences using *at*, *for*, *from*, *in*, *of* or *to*.

1 Shortages........critical components were a regular threat........the growth of the mobile phone market.

2 When the fire broke out........the plant, there were millions of chips, ready........shipment.

3 Damage........smoke and water contaminated all the stock.

4 Philips told Ericsson and Nokia that there would only be minor disruption........production.

5 Together, Ericsson and Nokia accounted........40 per cent of Philips' production.

6 Nokia immediately began checking the status........the five components that Philips supplied.

7 Their Japanese and US suppliers agreed to give them priority status........supplies........chips.

8 As a result........the fire, it is estimated that Philips lost $400m........sales.

9 Two of the suppliers agreed........lead times that were less than a week.

2 Look at the time prepositions in italic (1–3). Then match each preposition with its meaning (a–c).

1 ... *until* three days later. (line 18)   a) inside a period of time

2 *Within* two days ... (line 19)   b) not later than a particular time or date

3 *By the end of* March, ... (line 28)   c) happening up to a particular point in time and then stopping

3 Find another example in paragraphs H and I of each preposition in Exercise 2. Then write your own examples.

E Vocabulary development

Look through the article and the exercises for this unit and make a collection of at least five useful words and expressions for talking about each of these topics.

• production (e.g. *manufacturing plant, production levels*)
• disasters/unexpected problems (e.g. *fire, shortages of*)
• getting supplies (e.g. *supplies, single-source*)

OVER TO YOU

1 What lessons can be learnt from the Nokia case that would help other companies manage an unexpected disaster, such as a fire, and minimise disruption to the supply chain?

Write a set of guidelines, including the lessons from the handling of the fire at Philips and any other suggestions you have.

2 Research a company that has faced serious supply-chain disruption as a result of an unexpected disaster. Think about these questions.

• How well prepared was the company for this type of event?
• How did they discover the problem? / How quickly did they react?
• What action did they take to recover from the disruption?

Present your findings as a report or presentation.

Developments in global manufacturing and sourcing

This unit looks at trends in global manufacturing and sourcing.

Discuss these questions.

1 Many companies in the developed world have moved all or part of their operations to countries such as Brazil, Russia, India or China. What developments have made this possible?

2 What do companies see as the benefits of transferring all or part of their business overseas?

3 Do you think it has been a successful strategy? Why? / Why not?

4 Do you think the trend will continue?

A **Understanding the main points**

Read the article on the opposite page and say whether these statements are true (T) or false (F). Correct the false ones.

1 Reductions in labour costs in emerging countries made global manufacturing a real possibility for companies in the developed world.

2 Locating production in low-cost countries has resulted in big savings for companies.

3 Most companies have miscalculated the true cost of sourcing and manufacturing in countries a long way from their home markets.

4 Even in low-cost countries, there is a shortage of workers with the right skills.

5 Most companies with production in emerging countries have already returned home.

B **Understanding the details**

Read the article again and answer these questions.

1 The writers think many companies have underestimated the real cost of logistics for global manufacturing. What two examples do they give to support this view?

2 According to the writers, companies will find it more and more difficult to find cheap labour with the right skills in emerging countries. What evidence support this view in:
   a) Slovakia?
   b) India?
   c) China?

3 What predictions do the writers make about:
   a) trends in offshoring?
   b) the future location and size of plants?

Is global manufacturing losing its attraction?

by Arnoud De Meyer and
Matthias Holweg

A The argument for global sourcing and taking advantage of the lower cost of labour for manufacturing in Eastern Europe and the Bric countries – Brazil, Russia, India, China – was mainly based on the cost of transport, which decreased by a third between 1960 and 2000.

B However, in our research and others' research, we found that none of the companies that had gone global achieved all the cost efficiencies they had predicted. Some even found that 'offshoring' operations was more expensive than sourcing or manufacturing locally, and so have returned to their home country.

C The cost of logistics may be a lot more important than originally estimated. Proctor & Gamble management, for example, reported that the company's storage and transport costs were higher than the operating expenses of its factories abroad. Other companies found that the product cost was much lower, but the price for lower costs was often reduced quality.

D Companies make two common mistakes when deciding to source components from abroad. First, they only tend to calculate the 'static' cost of a supply chain. That is basically the cost per unit ex-supplier factory and the transport cost together. With global sourcing, the lower labour cost reduces the unit cost of the product. This generally offsets the higher transport cost of bringing it into the home market from China. Often companies ignore or underestimate other costs. An example of this is the additional cost for buffer stocks, as a long supply chain is less able to respond quickly to changes in demand.

E Second, companies often assume that costs remain stable and do not consider what we call 'dynamic' costs. The belief is that countries in Eastern Europe, China and India have an unlimited supply of low-cost labour. Although this is certainly still true for China and India, the reality is that these workers are not always trained to the necessary level. Finding the right staff can be a challenge.

F Car manufacturers relocating to Slovakia in Eastern Europe, for example, will find that the supply of trained workers has been almost exhausted and that wage inflation is rising fast as manufacturers compete for labour. In India, trained staff will change jobs several times per year if they see the chance of higher salaries elsewhere, and staff turnover of 20% has become normal. In China, a trained middle manager in the car sector, fluent in English and Mandarin, can earn more in Shanghai than in Wolfsburg or Birmingham.

G Our research suggests that manufacturing will increasingly come back to where the markets are. 'Backshoring', as we call it, does not mean that all manufacturing will come back. The emerging countries are also very large markets, and local production will still serve local consumption there. In the future, companies will need to think about having networks of smaller flexible plants that can produce customised products for local markets.

FT

C How the text is organised

What do these words refer to in the article?

1 they (line 30)
2 that (line 32)
3 this (line 37)
4 it (line 38)

5 this (line 41)
6 this (line 51)
7 these (line 52)
8 there (line 78)

VOCABULARY

A Definitions

Match the words and phrases from the article (1–10) with their meanings (a–j).

1	labour	a)	countries with less-developed economies that are expected to experience lots of growth
2	cost efficiencies	b)	the cost of an item at the supplier's factory, not including delivery charges
3	offshoring	c)	the rate at which people leave an organisation and are replaced by others
4	expenses	d)	all the people available to work in a country
5	ex-supplier factory	e)	a general rise in rates of pay, e.g. in a particular country
6	unit cost	f)	extra quantities of stock that are kept in case they are needed
7	buffer stocks	g)	when a company moves part of its operations to another, often cheaper country
8	wage inflation	h)	ways of saving money or wasting less money
9	staff turnover	i)	price per item
10	emerging countries	j)	money a company spends in order to operate

B Word partnerships

1 Match the adjectives (1–6) with the nouns (a–f) to make word partnerships from the article.

1	global	a)	labour
2	operating	b)	production/markets
3	low-cost	c)	expenses
4	trained	d)	products
5	local	e)	sourcing
6	customised	f)	staff/workers

2 Find at least three nouns in the article that can go before the noun *cost*, e.g. *production*.

3 Think of at least three more noun–noun word partnerships with *cost*.

C Sentence completion

Use words and phrases from Exercises A and B to complete these sentences.

1 Many companies are finding that g........ s........^{a} and manufacturing no longer make sense. One of the problems is high o........ e........^{b}. Another problem is increasing levels of w........ i........^{c}.

2 Even in e........ c........^{a} with l........-c........ l........^{b}, like China and India, there are signs that there are shortages of t........ w........^{c} with the right skills.

3 In the future, manufacturers may have smaller production units that will produce c........ p........^{a} to meet the needs of the l........ m........^{b}.

4 In order to ensure that a business always has the correct amount of stock, most companies hold b........ s.........

5 Manufacturers are constantly looking for ways to make their operations more efficient and achieve c........ e........ in their supply chains.

D Word search

Find words and phrases in the article which have a similar meaning.

1   calculated approximately (paragraph C)
2   usually do something (paragraph D)
3   balances (paragraph D)
4   do not to consider (paragraph D)
5   make an estimate that is too low (paragraph D)
6   believe something is true (paragraph E)
7   stay the same (paragraph E)
8   used up (paragraph F)

E Understanding expressions

Find these two terms in the article. Then choose the best explanation for each one (a–d).

1   'static' costs (line 31)
2   'dynamic' costs (line 47)

a) costs that are rising all the time
b) costs that are predictable and don't change a lot
c) costs that are fixed at a low price
d) costs that vary and are continuously changing

F Word families

1   Complete the chart.

noun: activity/ organisation	verb	adjective
........^{1}	to ....^{2}	offshored (production/ manufacturing)
operating / ....^{3}	to operate	........^{4} (costs/strategy)
........^{5}	to ....^{6}	sourced (components/products/services) ....^{7} (decision/strategy)
........^{8} / manufacture	to ....^{9}	manufacturing (plant/industry) ....^{10} (goods/products)

2   Write your own sentences with any of the words in Exercise 1 that are new to you or that you are unsure how to use.

OVER TO YOU

1   What are your predictions for the next five years for one of the following?
   • the offshoring of manufacturing to low-cost countries
   • the global sourcing of components, products and services
   • the organisation of manufacturing

2   If the trend for 'backshoring' manufacturing nearer to home markets continues, what are the implications for developing countries? Which ones will do better? Which ones will do worse?

3   Based on the information in the article and your own experience, prepare a checklist of points that companies need to consider when evaluating the business case for sourcing components from low-cost countries, far from the home market.

Outsourcing production to China

This unit examines the case for outsourcing manufacturing to China.

BEFORE YOU READ

Discuss these questions.

1   Many companies in more industrialised countries have outsourced manufacturing to China.
    a) Why have they taken this business decision?
    b) What are the potential risks?
    c) Do you think this trend will continue? Why? / Why not?
2   What other developing countries are becoming centres for global manufacturing?

READING

A   Understanding the main points

Read the article on the opposite page and answer these questions.

1   Which statement best sums up the main idea of the article?
    a) More and more manufacturers from industrialised countries will locate all their production in China.
    b) Most manufacturers will move all their production back from China to be nearer to their customers.
    c) Many manufacturers will continue locating their production in China, but only for certain types of products.
2   According to the writer, will China lose or keep its position as a top location for global manufacturing?
3   The article explains some problems manufacturers may face when setting up in China. Which three does the writer mention, and in what order?
    a) long distances from customers
    b) low productivity
    c) complex power structure at a provincial level
    d) lack of workers with the right skills
    e) increasing costs

B   Understanding details

Read the article again and answer these questions.

1   The writer gives two reasons to explain why China is a good location for manufacturers from industrialised countries. What are they?
2   How does the cost for workers compare in China and Singapore?
3   Why weren't China's low labour costs a key factor for Mr Goul when he decided where to locate his main plant?
4   Why did Johnson Controls have to set up joint ventures with five companies in China rather than just one?
5   Why doesn't locating production in China make sense for Hubbell, the US electronics manufacturer?

Foreign makers find advantages on home ground

by Peter Marsh

A Nik Seidenader, Managing Director of a German maker of inspection machines for the pharmaceuticals industry, thought about joining the rush of manufacturers to China last year, but decided against it. In India, Vikas Goel, Chairman of Esys, a computer company, decided to locate his main plant in Singapore.

B Behind the two men's strategic choices lies an important change affecting global manufacturing. Despite China's status as factory to the world, foreign companies are starting to think harder about whether to set up operations there. An awareness is growing that longer-established industrialised regions still have plenty to offer manufacturers, in spite of their higher labour costs.

C 'Although China will continue to be a strong competitor for many kinds of manufacturing investment, it is fair to say companies are re-evaluating their policies on investing there,' says Hal Sirkin, a manufacturing expert from the Boston Consulting Group.

D China still has a strong appeal for manufacturers. Not only does it offer an expanding market of 1bn-plus people, it is now also the world's third biggest manufacturer after the US and Japan. But there is increasing concern about the pitfalls of setting up operating plants in China.

E First, costs have generally risen, including labour costs and freight charges. Although labour in China may still remain cheap, that is not always the most important factor in a business's calculations. For Mr Goel, for instance, it was not important that Singapore's hourly labour charges are two-and-a-half times higher than China's: costs for labour in computer assembly account for less than two per cent of production costs.

F Operating in China's political system – with power shared among many provincial, state-owned organisations often competing with one another and with Beijing – can sometimes be a problem. Johnson Controls, the US car-parts company, had to set up five joint ventures with different state-owned companies – rather than the single operation the company would have liked – because it could not reach agreement with government officials in the different areas of the country.

G Finally, the main industrialised countries are rediscovering their competitive edge. Jim Womack, President of the Lean Enterprise Institute, says increasing numbers of companies make products whose specifications change frequently to meet shifts in demand. If factories are too far away from customers, it can be hard to react quickly to such changes. Tim Powers, Chief Executive of Hubbell, a US electrical products manufacturer that sells mainly in North America, says: 'Of our production, 40 per cent is customised. China is just too far away to make it useful for us as a manufacturing centre.'

H The best approach for many companies will be a 'hybridised' strategy. This means splitting production according to factors such as technical sophistication and closeness to markets – and choosing the location that makes most sense in each case. In some cases, China will be suitable; in others, it will not.

FT

C Understanding meaning

In paragraph H, the writer says that *The best approach for many companies will be a 'hybridised strategy' for their production.* What do you think this means? Select the best explanation.

a) Many companies will need to have one main strategy for locating all their production.
b) Many companies will need a mix of different strategies suitable for different parts of their production.

VOCABULARY

A Definitions

Match these words and phrases from the article (1–9) with their meanings (a–i).

1	labour costs	a)	belonging to or controlled by the government
2	freight	b)	a new business started by two or more companies
3	state-owned	c)	an advantage that a company has over its competitors
4	joint venture	d)	a detailed description of how a product should be made
5	officials	e)	quality of being more advanced and complex than others
6	competitive edge	f)	costs associated with employing people
7	specifications	g)	goods transported by road, rail and air
8	customised	h)	people with positions of authority in an organisation
9	sophistication	i)	specifically made to meet the needs of the customer

B Word partnerships

1 Match the adjectives (1–4) with the nouns (a–d).

1	global	a)	regions/countries
2	industrialised	b)	sophistication
3	state-owned	c)	organisations/companies
4	technical	d)	manufacturing

2 Find nouns in the article that follow these nouns.

1 manufacturing (3 nouns)
2 freight/labour (2 nouns)
3 government
4 operating

C Text completion

Use word partnerships from Exercises A and B to complete this text.

Production costs have increased in China, reflecting higher energy and commodity prices. Even l........ c........[1] are rising, especially for more skilled workers.

As a result, companies from the main i........ c........[2] are thinking carefully before deciding to set up o........ p........[3] in China and are looking for countries with lower costs, especially those producing products with low levels of t........ s........[4].

Will this mean less m........ i........[5] in China?

Is China is in danger of losing its c........ e........[6] as a centre for g........ m........[7]?

Will higher f........ c........[8] and other costs make it more attractive for manufacturers to set up nearer to their home markets?

D Word search

1 Find words or phrases in the article with a similar meaning.

   1 position (paragraph B)
   2 to establish (paragraph B)
   3 attraction (paragraph D)
   4 worry (paragraph D)
   5 unexpected difficulties (paragraph D)
   6 just one (paragraph F)
   7 changes (paragraph G)
   8 dividing (paragraph H)
   9 is the most a sensible thing to do (paragraph H)

2 Find an adjective in paragraph D that gives the idea of 'getting bigger'.

3 Think of at least three adjectives with the opposite meaning.

E Sentence completion

Use words from Exercise D1 in the correct form to complete these sentences.

1 If we decide to outsource production, we need to select a supply company which is flexible enough to meet .... in demand.

2 When we started sourcing components from India, one of the biggest .... was long delays at customs.

3 I can see the .... of keeping all our production here, but my .... is the shortage of skilled labour.

4 If companies need to react quickly to changes in demand, it doesn't .... to locate production far away from their main markets.

5 The plan is to .... a joint venture with a local distribution company.

6 Our plan is to .... production between our plants in Mexico and our plant in Atlanta.

OVER TO YOU

1 In the current economic climate, do you think the trend for shifting production to countries with lower costs in Eastern European, Asia and Latin America will grow or decline? Will it vary depending on the sector?

   Give a presentation of your conclusions.

2 Prepare a short report or presentation, making the case for or against outsourcing all or part of its production to China for:
   a) a fashion retailer
   b) a car manufacturer
   c) a toy manufacturer.

3 Choose a developing country. Research the country and prepare a set of guidelines to help companies when deciding whether to relocate or set up production there.

Ethical sourcing

This unit offers different expert views about how companies can manage the risk to their business of unethical practices in supplier companies.

BEFORE YOU READ

Discuss these questions.

1   What are the risks for brand owners and retailers of negative publicity about conditions in its suppliers' factories abroad?

2   Most companies have codes of labour practice to ensure acceptable working conditions for all workers in its supply chain. What action can they take to:
   • make sure suppliers and their subcontractors follow the code?
   • deal with suppliers who fail to comply with the code?
   • improve conditions for workers in its suppliers' factories long term?

READING

A   Understanding the main points

Read the article on the opposite page and answer these questions.

1   What unethical practices were discovered at:
   a) Primark's three supplier factories in India?
   b) Tesco's supplier in Bangladesh?
2   What action did Primark take?
3   Which two experts give practical suggestions for improving auditing at supplier factories?
4   Which expert gives an example of a company with a successful system for auditing its suppliers?

B   Understanding details

Read the article again and say whether these statements summarise the views of the supply-chain expert (S), the academic (A) or the executive (E).

1   Demand from retailers for cheap clothes makes it more likely that suppliers in developing countries will use cheap child labour.
2   Sacking suppliers is not the solution, as it can lead to even worse conditions for workers.
3   On their own, external audits are not an effective way of improving labour practices.
4   The problem of child labour will not go away until the economies of developing countries become stronger.
5   Supplier factories are more likely to improve working practices if they can see the benefits for them.
6   One good strategy for companies is to put their own people in suppliers' factories to audit and help them improve conditions.
7   The priority for companies today is the improvement of conditions for workers in subcontractors' factories and for home workers.

Moral dilemma for retailers dependent on suppliers in developing countries

THE PROBLEM

A Primark, the clothing retailer, last month announced it had fired three suppliers in India after it was dis-
5 covered that they had subcontracted work to home workers who used child labour. George Weston, Chief Executive of Associated British Foods, which owns Primark, claimed that
10 the factories had been involved in 'systematic deception' and that regular audits had failed to uncover the violations.

B Tesco, the UK retailer, faces alle-
15 gations of neglect of factory workers after a report from the charity War on Want said that its researchers found workers in a factory in Bangalore being paid 'half a living wage'.

C Is it possible for companies with suppliers in developing countries to guarantee that their goods have been produced in conditions that are ethically acceptable? And what kind of 25 audit system could provide consumers with such a guarantee?

SUPPLY-CHAIN EXPERT

D As retail companies continue to push prices down, then clothing factories,
30 working on small margins, are going to try and cut costs – and that can mean they employ child labour because it's cheap. No one with any experience of supply chains in Asia will be sur-
35 prised that regular audits did not expose violations.

E Companies need to move away from simplistic, unreliable inspections towards building trust with their sup-
40 pliers. That means working together to develop good corporate social responsibility practices rather than just carrying out spot checks. It also means getting suppliers to see that acceptable
45 employment practices are in their interest and helping them to develop the policies and practices that will make them a trusted supplier. Simply cancelling the contracts with factories that
50 indirectly employ children has the potential to make a bad situation worse. Where are those children now, I wonder?

ACADEMIC

F Studies show that auditing suppliers
55 has already had a real impact on improving ethical practices in developing countries. The problem has now moved to the level of subcontractors and work done inside homes. But the
60 problem of child labour in developing countries can only be solved through economic development that gives children real alternatives. Poor parents in India, Pakistan or Vietnam
65 cannot choose between sending their children to a school or a factory. The real choice is between eating or going hungry.

EXECUTIVE

G It is possible to guarantee ethical working conditions. But companies need to take an active role in the manufacturing process rather than relying on independent auditors who visit occasionally.
75 Applica markets and distributes kitchen and home products, and its products are manufactured mainly in China and Mexico. It has long-standing strategic partnerships with most of its manufac-
80 turers. All must adhere to quality controls and codes of conduct, including social responsibility. Engineers and marketers from Applica spend a large amount of time with these manufactur-
85 ers. They also have on-site teams whose task is to audit the manufacturers and work with them to ensure that quality and ethical practices are maintained.

FT

VOCABULARY

A Definitions

Find words or phrases in the article which match these meanings.

1 deliberately hiding the truth (paragraph A)
2 failures to obey regulations (paragraph A)
3 statements accusing a company of misconduct (paragraph B)
4 lack of necessary care (paragraph B)
5 a wage sufficient for a worker to support a family and buy things they need to live (paragraph B)
6 to make it certain that something will happen (paragraph C)
7 differences between the cost price and the selling price (paragraph D)
8 official examinations of labour practices (paragraph D)
9 processes of running a business in a way that helps people in society to improve their quality of life (paragraph E)
10 quick, unplanned inspections (paragraph E)
11 sets of rules for ethical behaviour that suppliers must follow (paragraph G)
12 based in the manufacturer's offices (paragraph G)

B Word partnerships

Match these words to make noun–noun partnerships from the article.

1	home	a)	practices
2	child	b)	conditions
3	audit	c)	labour
4	employment	d)	system
5	working	e)	controls
6	quality	f)	workers

C Word search

Find verbs in the article with a similar meaning which can replace the verbs in italic.

1 Independent auditors officially *inspect* each supplier four times a year.
2 Our own compliance team also *conducts* spot checks during visits to suppliers.
3 If an audit *uncovers* minor violations, we work with the supplier to solve the problem.
4 For more serious violations, *terminating* the contract is often the only solution.
5 Last year, we had to *get rid of* [a] two suppliers. They had made no attempt to *comply with* [b] our code of employment and had *made use of* [c] child labour, despite warnings.

D **Sentence completion**

Use the words in the box to complete these sentences.

| allegations audits auditors child labour code employment practices |
| ethical inspections living wage subcontractors working conditions |

1 Valmark Sports is fighting to save its reputation after more ....[a] of ethically unacceptable ....[b] in its supply chain last month.

2 Target has a full-time compliance team of 40 staff, including more than 20 foreign-based ....

3 The audit team carries out 100% of its official factory .... inspections unannounced.

4 The aim of the audit system is to ensure consistency of .... working practices in all the company's supply factories.

5 Our ....[a] of employment standards includes provisions to ensure that ....[b] are safe, workers are paid a ....[c] and that no ....[d] is used.

6 We conduct regular ....[a] of both our primary suppliers and also smaller ....[b].

E **Prepositions**

Complete the sentences using the prepositions in the box.

| down in in in in of on to with with |

1 Companies must be prepared to take an active role ....[a] improving working practices ....[b] their supply chains.

2 It's not enough to rely .... random inspections and audits.

3 Constantly pushing ....[a] prices and lead times will make it harder for supply companies to adhere ....[b] a manufacturer's codes ....[c] conduct.

4 A better strategy is to develop strategic partnerships .... your primary suppliers.

5 Don't expect immediate changes; it takes time to build trust .... supply companies.

6 Show suppliers that it is ....[a] their interest to improve working conditions ....[b] their factories.

OVER TO YOU

1 What are the benefits for suppliers in developing countries that invest time and resources in improving conditions for their workers?

2 Prepare a short report or presentation to persuade a supplier that it is in its interest to improve conditions for its workers.

3 Research a company that has had a lot of negative publicity because of unethical working practices in a supplier's workplace. Write a short report explaining:

- what happened
- what action the company has taken, with what results
- what other companies can learn from the case.

Transporting fresh produce

This unit describes how fresh fruit and vegetables are delivered to supermarket shelves.

BEFORE YOU READ

Discuss these questions.

1 What do you think is the shortest time for fresh fruit and vegetables to be delivered to a supermarket shelf from the moment the order is placed?
2 How do you think fresh fruit and vegetables are transported to ensure they arrive in good condition?

READING

A Understanding the main points

Read the article on the opposite page and answer these questions.

1 What is meant by the phrase in the article *making India in England* (line 8)?
2 What is meant by the phrase *cool chain* (line 18)?
3 In what way is organic food different from other food products?
4 What are important factors for keeping organic food products fresh when transporting them?
5 How quickly can fresh produce be transported from the farm to the supermarket shelf?

B Understanding details

Read the article again and answer these questions.

1 What is the name of the modern equipment used to transport fresh fruit and vegetables? Why do you think it is called that?
2 What does reefer technology control?
3 What functions do microprocessors control in modern refrigerated containers?
4 What are the steps in the process when a retail chain orders fresh produce from suppliers?
5 What kind of fresh produce is transported by plane rather than by ship?
6 Where is BA's World Cargo Perishable Handling Centre located?
7 Which company runs the centre?
8 How much fresh produce does it handle each year?
9 What kind of activities take place at the centre?
10 How were things different 10 to 15 years ago?

A very tight supply chain

by Sarah Murray

A 'Even mangoes can be got in England now,' declares Cyril Fielding, the college principal in E.M. Forster's novel *A Passage to India*. 'They ship them in
5 ice-cold rooms. You can make India in England apparently, just as you can make England in India.'

B Today, making India in England is even easier with the help of atmos-
10 phere-controlled refrigerated containers, known as *reefers*, monitored by computer chips. But while transport equipment is now highly sophisticated, the delivery of fresh fruit and
15 vegetables also relies on extremely complex logistics systems which are designed to cut every last hour out of the 'cool chain'.

C Certainly, the containers themselves
20 have moved on since the 'ice-cold rooms' described by Cyril Fielding. Reefer technology can control everything from temperature and humidity to ventilation and gas levels. Micropro-
25 cessors in reefers detect temperature or other problems and fix them during the voyage, sending alerts to the vessel's bridge or to a website through which shippers can make
30 adjustments remotely.

D These new technologies are increasingly important, as the demand for organic food grows. To satisfy demand, retailers are looking beyond national
35 borders – and organic food is more time sensitive than conventional produce. 'You just have to be much more conscious of temperature fluctuations, making sure those are minimised, that
40 the ventilation setting is properly adjusted and that the transit time isn't too long,' says Barbara Pratt, Chairman of the US International Refrigerated Transportation Association.

E Speed is crucial for perishable produce, particularly given the growing popularity of 'fresh-cut' produce – pieces of fruit, vegetables and salad that are washed, peeled, trimmed and
50 ready to eat, but which have a far shorter shelf life than whole produce.

F In the past five years, UK retailers have dramatically reduced the time it takes to get fresh produce on the super-
55 market shelf. Today, an order placed by a retail chain might be sent that evening to the suppliers, who start the picking and packing the following morning and send the produce to the
60 distribution centre that evening, allowing the goods to appear on the shelves the following morning. 'That's a very condensed supply chain,' says Brian Gaunt of Christian Salvesen's
65 food and consumer division.

G The use of aviation has also speeded up the perishables supply chain and brought new items to the supermarkets, particularly high-value produce such
70 as soft fruit from the US, South Africa and Zimbabwe.

H Many of these and other airfreighted fruit and vegetables are processed at the British Airways World Cargo Per-
75 ishables Handling Centre at Heathrow Airport. The centre, which is operated by Christian Salvesen, is a chilled facility of almost 70,000 square feet that processes more than 90,000 tonnes
80 of perishable cargo each year.

I At the centre, bulk shipments are broken up into individual orders and sorted by product type or according to the regional distribution centre for
85 which they are destined. Machines at the centre print branded labels for each retailer, including the weight, sell-by date and price, allowing supermarkets to change their prices at the last minute.

J 'If you go back 10 to 15 years, typically there would have been three to four handling points in the supply chain – whether at origin or in destination,' says Gerry Mundy, BA's Global
95 Perishables Manager. 'All that is now handled by the perishable handling centre.'

FT

VOCABULARY

A Definitions

Find words and phrases in the article which match these meanings.

1 checked and controlled (paragraph B)

m........

2 notice something that is not easy to see, hear, etc. (paragraph C)

d........

3 warning signals, usually visible or audible (paragraph C)

a........

4 small changes made to a machine (paragraph C)

a........

5 frequent changes, especially from high to low or low to high (paragraph D)

f........

6 the time needed to transport goods (paragraph D)

t........ t........

7 describes food that can become bad quickly (paragraph E)

p........

8 food that is obtained through farming, especially in large quantities (paragraph E)

p........

9 length of time food products will stay in good condition once they are put on sale (paragraph E)

s........ l........

10 shortened, concentrated (paragraph F)

c........

11 kept cool, at a low temperature (but not frozen) (paragraph H)

c........

12 deliveries in large quantities (paragraph I)

b........ s........

13 last date at which a food product can be sold (paragraph I)

s........-b........ d........

B Verbs and prepositions

Find verb + preposition phrases in the article which match these meanings.

1 is dependent on (paragraph B)

2 remove from (paragraph B)

3 become more modern (paragraph C)

4 searching outside (paragraph D)

5 made quicker (paragraph G)

6 divided into smaller units (paragraph I)

C **Word partnerships**

1 Match these words to make noun–noun partnerships from the article.

1	computer	a)	fluctuations
2	transport	b)	centre
3	logistics	c)	life
4	temperature	d)	centre
5	transit	e)	systems
6	shelf	f)	type
7	distribution	g)	equipment
8	consumer	h)	time
9	handling	i)	chips
10	product	j)	division

2 Match the verbs (1–7) with the nouns (a–g) to form phrases used in the article.

1	to control	a)	adjustments
2	to detect	b)	prices
3	to make	c)	demand
4	to satisfy	d)	labels
5	to place	e)	a problem
6	to print	f)	the temperature
7	to change	g)	an order

D **Sentence completion**

Use the correct form of phrases from Exercise C2 to complete these sentences.

1 During the transport of fresh produce, it is important to . . . . carefully.

2 Fresh, organic fruit and vegetables are flown halfway across the world to . . . . consumer . . . .

3 In modern containers, if . . . . such as temperature fluctuations are . . . . , microprocessors can automatically . . . .

4 The supply chain for fresh produce is so well organised, fruit and vegetables can be on the supermarket shelf within two days of an . . . . being . . . .

5 The BA World Cargo Perishables Handling Centre is so sophisticated, machines can . . . . for each retailer, which means the retailer can decide to . . . . up to the last minute.

OVER TO YOU

1 The article describes how perishable produce is brought to supermarket shelves in as fresh a condition as possible. With many consumers concerned about food miles (how far food has to travel from its source to our tables), how do you see the future of the transport and distribution systems described in the article?

2 Some people argue that flying fruit and vegetables from Africa to Europe is bad for the environment and should be reduced. Others argue that growing these crops for export to rich countries is an important source of income for farmers in developing countries. Which opinion do you agree with? Why?

The impact of higher energy costs

This unit considers the impact of higher energy costs on Procter & Gamble's distribution system.

Discuss these questions.

1 How should companies with big distribution networks react to the increase in energy costs?

2 In the light of current and future environmental and energy issues, what challenges are companies likely to face when operating their supply chains?

3 Which production and distribution model do you think will be adopted by companies in the future – large, regional production sites with centralised warehouses, or smaller production sites with smaller warehouses nearer to the customer? Why?

READING

A ### Understanding the main points

Read the article on the opposite page and answer these questions.

1 How has Procter & Gamble's (P&G's) production and distribution system been organised over the last 20 years?

2 What kind of study is P&G now carrying out?

3 What factors is P&G taking into account in its study?

B ### Understanding details

Read the article again and answer these questions.

1 What is one way P&G would be able to cut its transportation bill?

2 When was P&G's current supply chain developed?

3 What was the price of oil at that time?

4 How does Keith Harrison describe what has happened to P&G's supply-chain design?

5 What is the main aim of the study started by P&G?

6 What supply-chain trends will P&G look at in its study?

7 What questions will P&G ask in the study?

8 What does Keith Harrison mean when he describes P&G's current supply chain as *large single-category regional production sites with long supply chains*?

9 At what point did P&G have to rethink its distribution strategy?

10 How have increased transport costs changed P&G's thinking about how it distributes goods?

11 P&G is the world's largest shipper of consumer goods. What figures support this?

12 What does Keith Harrison mean by the phrase *distribution-cost equation*?

Oil price forces P&G to rethink its distribution

by Jonathan Birchall and Elizabeth Rigby

A Soaring energy prices are forcing Procter & Gamble, the world's biggest consumer goods company, to rethink how it distributes products and to
5 consider shifting manufacturing sites closer to consumers to cut its transport bill.

B Keith Harrison, Head of Global Supply at P&G, the maker of Tide deter-
10 gent, Crest toothpaste and Pampers nappies, said the era of high oil prices was forcing P&G to change. 'A lot of our supply-chain design work was really developed and implemented in
15 the 1980s and 1990s, when our capital spending on capacity was fairly high, and oil was $10 a barrel,' said Mr Harrison. 'I could say that the supply-chain design is now upside down. The envi-
20 ronment has changed. Transportation cost is going to create an even more distributed sourcing network than we would have had without the big rise in oil prices.'

C A couple of years ago, P&G launched a comprehensive review of the design

of its supply operations, in response both to rising energy costs and its increasingly global expansion. 'We've
30 kicked off a study that really asks: what is our business going to look like in 2015?' Mr Harrison said.

D The study will include assessing trends such as reductions in product
35 size, sustainable packaging and future consumer demand based on regions. It will also try to anticipate changes in the global operating environment. 'What happens if oil is $200 a barrel? What
40 happens if you can't ship using trucks on the weekends or if there are road-congestion issues? Or if you can't bring trucks into cities any more?'

E Mr Harrison, responsible for the
45 supply chain behind P&G's global sales of more than $80bn, said its supply system was based on 'large single-category regional production sites with long supply chains'. 'Up to
50 where oil was $70 or so, it was hard to justify building new capacity only on the back of new distribution costs. But with oil going as high as $140, the world has changed.'

F The company is the world's largest shipper of consumer goods, with an estimated 30,000 trucks on the road around the world every day. It also operates 145 manufacturing plants.

G Mr Harrison said high energy costs were already changing the calculations affecting the siting of factories. As an example, he quoted a babycare plant being built to meet growing demand in
65 China, located at Xiqing in the northern province of Tianjin, rather than at an existing facility near Guangzhou in southern China. 'Part of the justification to go to Xiqing was distribution
70 costs. Part was that I needed more capacity. But today's distribution-cost equation could lead you to a different answer than you might have reached otherwise.'

FT

C **Searching for figures**

What do these figures refer to?

a) $10

b) 2015

c) $200

d) $80bn

e) $70

f) $140

g) 30,000

h) 145

VOCABULARY

A Definitions

Find words or phrases in the article which match these meanings.

1 increasing rapidly (paragraph A)
2 to think again about something in order to change or improve it (paragraph A)
3 moving, relocating (paragraph A)
4 to reduce (paragraph A)
5 a period of time that is marked by particular events (paragraph B)
6 put into operation (paragraph B)
7 investment of money in business assets (paragraph B)
8 factories and warehouses (paragraph B)
9 completely different from before (paragraph B)
10 a study of something to see where improvements can be made (paragraph C)
11 started, launched (paragraph C)
12 to imagine or expect what will happen, sometimes taking action in preparation (paragraph D)
13 when there is too much traffic on the roads (paragraph D)
14 to give a good reason for doing something (paragraph E)
15 locating, positioning something (paragraph G)

B Sentence completion

Use the words and phrases from Exercise A to complete these sentences.

1 P&G is considering .... manufacturing sites closer to consumers because of .... energy prices
2 It believes the .... of cheap oil is finished for ever.
3 The company is having to .... its entire supply-chain system.
4 It has just .... a study which will try to .... how the global environment will change in the next five to 10 years.
5 The study will also consider traffic issues such as ....
6 When the oil price was below US $70 a barrel, it was difficult to .... building new plants based only on transport costs.
7 In the future, the .... of new plants will have to take transport costs into account.
8 P&G's current supply-chain system was planned and .... in the 1980s and 1990s.
9 Depending on the results of the .... it is carrying out, P&G will change the way it organises its supply-chain system.
10 P&G needs to .... what it spends on transporting goods.
11 Because of big increases in the oil price, the design of the supply chain is now ...., compared to the previous two decades.
12 In the 1980s and '90s, P&G had high levels of ...., when it was building its supply-chain system.
13 The 1980s and '90s were a period of rapid growth for P&G, so it needed to spend money on new .... for the production and storage of goods.

C Word partnerships

Match these words to make noun–noun partnerships from the article. Sometimes more than one combination is possible, and some words can be used twice.

1	energy	a)	costs
2	consumer	b)	plants
3	manufacturing	c)	prices
4	transport	d)	operations
5	oil	e)	goods
6	capital	f)	sites
7	transportation	g)	demand
8	operating	h)	cost
9	product	i)	spending
10	production	j)	environment
11	distribution	k)	bill
12	supply	l)	size

D Word families

1 What are the verbs that come from these nouns?

1 distribution
2 manufacturing
3 production
4 consumer
5 transportation
6 spending
7 expansion
8 calculations

2 What are the nouns that come from these verbs?

1 implement
2 develop
3 assess
4 reduce
5 justify
6 ship
7 operate
8 locate

E Word search

Find five words or phrases in the article which mean *a place where products are manufactured*.

OVER TO YOU

1 Do you think P&G and similar companies will change their supply systems away from large, single-category regional production sites? What would be the advantages and disadvantages of doing so?

2 Imagine you are the head of logistics or supply-chain management at a large international manufacturer of consumer goods. Use the information in the article and other research to prepare and give a presentation to the executive board of the company about the need to rethink the company's supply-chain system.

A new distribution model

This unit considers how supply chains will need to change in the future as a result of higher energy prices and concerns about carbon emissions.

BEFORE YOU READ

Discuss these questions.

1   What are some traditional strategies and aims of running supply chains?
2   What new factors will companies have to take into account when designing their supply chains?
3   In what ways can a company reduce transport costs in its supply chain?
4   Think of as many ways as possible to reduce carbon emissions in freight transport.

READING

A   Understanding the main points

Read the article on the opposite page and answer these questions.

1   What examples are given of traditional strategies for the organisation of supply chains?
2   What is the likely future strategy for the organisation of supply chains?
3   What are the factors pushing this new strategy?

B   Understanding details

Read the article again and say whether these statements are true (T), false (F) or there is not enough information (N). Give your reasons.

1   Traditional supply-chain strategies were not greatly concerned about transport costs or carbon emissions.
2   Many companies are now against building huge warehouses because they are damaging to the environment.
3   Just-in-time, lean manufacturing and low-cost country sourcing are part of the new supply-chain strategy.
4   Tipping-point analysis argues that goods should always be stored close to the customer.
5   Products such as soft drinks or paper will continue to be delivered on a just-in-time basis.
6   Kimberly-Clark is the leader in moving its distribution centres closer to customers.
7   It is more energy efficient to have big, centralised warehouses rather than small, local ones.
8   Most ways of reducing carbon emissions in freight transport come at the expense of higher costs.
9   Shared warehouses and shared deliveries will be the model for the future.
10 This new model will give improved on-shelf availability.

Finding better ways to deliver the goods

by Rod Newing

A Increased transport costs due to oil-price rises can change the economics on which supply chains were built.

B Traditional strategies were aimed
5 at reducing the amount of money tied up in inventory and the number of warehouses. However, this was often at the expense of increased frequency of deliveries and longer transport dis-
10 tances, and therefore higher emissions.

C Strategies, such as just-in-time, lean manufacturing and even low-cost country sourcing, must be re-evaluated in the light of fuel prices. We have
15 entered a new era where different supply-chain strategies are needed to produce high performance, says *Past the Tipping Point*, a recent report from Accenture and Ilog, a French business-
20 software company.

D Jonathan Wright, a supply chain consultant at Accenture, explains that tipping-point analysis is an end-to-end assessment of the supply chain.
25 The aim is to understand at what point inventory should be held further forward in the supply chain to reduce transport costs.

E Moving inventory closer to demand
30 lowers transport and emissions at the expense of higher inventory costs. 'The tipping point occurs at different fuel prices, depending on the type and nature of the product,' he says. 'The
35 tipping point will be lower with a low-cost bulky product, such as soft drinks or paper. There will always be areas where just-in-time is the right thing to do and others where it is history.'

F Kimberly-Clark's *Network of the Future* places distribution centres closer to its key customers and markets, reducing the number of delivery trips. Its strategy aims for 70 per cent of
45 products to be made and sold in the same country. In the US alone in 2007, it saved nearly 2.8m miles and 500,000 gallons of fuel.

G There is usually a carbon trade-
50 off between more energy-efficient, centralised warehouses and transport costs, but, generally, cost and carbon reduction go together.

H Professor Alan McKinnon, Director
55 of the Logistics Research Centre at Scotland's Heriot-Watt University, has identified nine ways of reducing carbon in freight transport, most of which will also reduce costs. These are: switch
60 from road and air to rail or water; reduce the number of links in supply chains; reduce average journey length; increase average vehicle loading; reduce empty running; increase vehicle
65 capacity; reschedule deliveries to off-peak periods; use more fuel-efficient vehicles; and use lower carbon fuels.

I Sharing distribution centres and deliveries is a powerful way to reduce
70 cost and carbon footprint. Judy Blackburn, Head of the UK Logistics team at consultancy Kurt Salmon Associates, says that when two competing companies have merged their logistics
75 operations and vehicle deliveries, transport costs have fallen by 15 to 25 per cent, saving 300,000–400,000 tonnes of carbon dioxide.

J 'Current supply-chain designs are
80 primarily aimed at improving on-shelf availability, reducing cost and supporting sound financial figures,' according to *The 2016 Future Supply Chain: Serving Consumers in a Sustainable
85 Way*, a report by the Global Commerce Initiative of manufacturers and retailers and Capgemini, the consultancy firm. 'In future, the industry must design for additional parameters, such as
90 reduction in CO_2 emissions, reduced energy consumption, and reduced traffic congestion.'

K The report forecasts that finished products will be shipped to shared
95 warehouses in which multiple manufacturers store their products. Shared transport will deliver to city hubs and regional consolidation centres. Final distribution to stores,
100 pick-up points and homes will use consolidated deliveries.

FT

VOCABULARY

A Definitions

Find words or phrases in the article which match these meanings.

1 locked away (so that it can't be used for anything else) (paragraph B)
2 considering (paragraph C)
3 from start to finish (paragraph D)
4 the moment when one particular result of a process becomes the most likely one, after a period when the result was not sure (paragraph E)
5 taking up a lot of space (paragraph E)
6 an acceptable balance between two very different things (paragraph G)
7 the extent to which a truck has a full load (paragraph H)
8 when trucks travel without carrying goods (paragraph H)
9 less busy times of day for travelling (paragraph H)
10 the amount of carbon emissions an activity produces (paragraph I)
11 joined part of their operations together (paragraph I)
12 factors, limits on how much should be allowed (paragraph J)
13 when several deliveries are combined together (paragraph K)

B Sentence completion

Use the words and phrases from Exercise A to complete these sentences.

1 It is expensive to store .... products in a warehouse, as they take up a lot of space.
2 For environmental reasons, most transport companies are trying to reduce their ....
3 One way to reduce carbon emissions is to deliver in ....-........ periods, when there is less traffic.
4 Another way is to avoid ...., when trucks return to a warehouse with no goods.
5 A third way is to increase average .... by making sure that trucks have as full a load as possible.
6 The traditional strategy of supply chains was to avoid having too much capital .... in inventory.
7 Supply chains in the future will have to take new .... into account, such as carbon emissions and road congestion.
8 In the planning of distribution systems, it is often necessary to make a ....-........ between inventory costs and transport costs.
9 In the future, deliveries from different suppliers will be .... so that trucks can carry full loads.
10 Some companies have .... their logistics operations in order to reduce transport costs.
11 The .... of when it is cheaper to store goods closer to the customer rather than using just-in-time delivery depends on the transport cost and the type of product.
12 The company had to rethink its supply chain strategy .... new developments in just-in-time management.
13 The consultant carried out an ........-........-........ assessment of the supply chain to understand more clearly the impact of holding inventory.

C   Prepositions

Complete the phrases from the article using the prepositions in the box.

at   at   between   by   from   in   in   of   of   on   on   to   to   to   to

1   the economics .... which supply chains were built.

2   the amount of money tied up .... inventory

3   .... the expense .... increased transport frequencies

4   .... the light .... fuel prices.

5   to understand .... what point inventory should be held further forward in the supply chain

6   depending .... the type and nature of the product

7   places distribution centres closer .... its key customers

8   a trade-off .... more energy-efficient, centralised warehouses and transport costs

9   switch .... road and air .... rail or water

10 reschedule deliveries .... off-peak periods

11 transport costs have fallen .... 15 to 20 per cent

12 final distribution .... stores, pick-up points and homes will use consolidated deliveries.

D   Definitions

1   Match the sentence halves to form definitions.

1 A method of production that aims to cut costs by producing ...	a) ... from areas of the world where manufacturing costs are lower.
2 The activity of finding and buying materials, parts or products ...	b) ... where things are done, supplied or made only when they are needed.
3 A system, especially for manufacturing, ...	c) ... only the quantity of goods that has been ordered and by reducing the amount of time and space that the production process uses.

2   Match each definition from Exercise 1 with the strategy for reducing the costs of production that it describes.

i)   just-in-time

ii) lean manufacturing

iii) low-cost country sourcing

OVER TO YOU

1   Look at the nine ways of reducing carbon emissions in freight transport mentioned by Professor McKinnon in the article. Pick the three which you think will be most effective and give your reasons.

2   To what extent do you agree with the findings of the report *The 2016 Future Supply Chain* that, in future, companies will use shared warehouses close to customers and deliveries will be consolidated? Give your reasons.

Managing changes in demand

This unit looks at the challenge of dealing with unexpected increases in demand and suggests ways companies can manage it.

BEFORE YOU READ

Discuss these questions.

1 What can cause temporary increases in demand for retail products? Which are predicable, e.g. a national holiday period? Which are unpredictable, e.g. unexpected popularity of a new toy or gadget?

2 What are the consequences if a company isn't able to deal with sudden changes in demand for its products, e.g. product shortages, obsolete stock?

3 What can a company do to make sure its supply chain can handle variations in demand?

READING

A Understanding the main points

1 Read the article on the opposite page and choose the best option to complete each statement.

1 Forecasting demand is especially difficult for *all products at Christmas / new products that become very popular.*

2 According to the writer, shortages of 'must-have' products are common at Christmas because manufacturers *underestimate demand / deliberately restrict stock to get interest.*

3 The writer *doesn't see / sees* product shortages as a serious risk for companies.

4 The best way for ensuring companies have the right stock levels to meet demand is *more accurate forecasting / making their supply chains more flexible.*

2 The article offers four main solutions for dealing with increases in demand. In what order are they mentioned?

a) Better communication of information between everyone in the supply chain
b) Supplier contracts with guarantees to increase production at short notice
c) Increasing the number of suppliers
d) More accurate forecasting for a better picture of demand for components

B Understanding details

Read the article again and answer these questions.

1 According to the article, what are three risks for companies associated with product shortages?

2 Why does Hewlett-Packard have two different plants for making Deskjet printers for the US market?

3 How much advanced warning must Jabil Circuit give its suppliers if they need to increase production by
a) 25 per cent?   b) 100 per cent?

4 What actions do Toyota and Dell take to make sure information on production levels is available to others in the supply chain?

Make sure you have your Christmas stock in

by Alison Maitland

A Every year at Christmas, much-advertised products disappear from the shelves long before most people have done their Christmas shopping, leaving consumers disappointed and frustrated.

B Forecasting the right quantity of a product and getting it to the right place at the right time is a tough challenge for businesses, especially when the item is new. 'It is the exciting products that are hard to forecast,' says Martin Smith, Head of the Manufacturing Industries Practice at PA Consulting.

C The continuation of pre-Christmas sell-outs, despite the use of sophisticated forecasting tools, has led to suspicions that companies ration the supply or even withhold 'must-have' goods to create interest among consumers. PA Consulting's Martin Smith thinks this is unlikely. 'If companies run out of stock, it won't help them maximise the profits they can make from a new product.'

D But Yossi Sheffi, Director of Massachusetts Institute of Technology's Centre for Transportation and Logistics, says it is not unusual for companies to announce expected shortages when launching a new product. 'People want more of something that is scarce. Most manufacturers will give newspapers these stories because they increase demand and help future sales.'

E But the danger is that actual shortages, especially in the period up to Christmas, will alienate customers, as well as lose potential sales. Another risk of running out of a 'must-have' product is that when supplies start again, the fashion may have passed. This can leave companies with unwanted stock.

F Getting stock levels right is not so much about perfecting forecasts as about building flexibility into the supply chain. Where possible, that means broadening the supply base so that manufacturers can step up production quickly in different locations, and use components from different sources.

G According to Professor Sheffi, one example of this kind of multi-sourcing is Hewlett-Packard. HP makes Deskjet printers for North America in plants in Vancouver and Singapore. Vancouver is more flexible and closer to the market, but more costly. So HP gives stable, high-volume production to Singapore and uses Vancouver to meet temporary surges in demand.

H Agreeing flexible contracts with suppliers is another solution that enables companies to increase or decrease production rapidly. Jabil Circuit, a US electronic manufacturing services company, requires suppliers to be able to boost deliveries by 25 per cent with a week's notice, and by 100 per cent with four weeks' notice.

I Forecasting can be made more accurate by collecting together predictions of customer demand across a wide region rather than responding on a store-by-store basis, according to Professor Sheffi. By using common components in different products, companies can also put together their forecasts for these products to give a more accurate picture of demand for the parts.

J A responsive supply chain depends on good communication between all its participants. In companies that do this well, there is a free flow of information, says Professor Sheffi. 'For example, Toyota displays continuous production reports in its plants, and Dell updates managers hourly on production.'

FT

VOCABULARY

A Definitions

1 Match these words and phrases from the article (1–10) with their meanings (a–j).

1	forecasting	a)	cause to dislike
2	sell-outs	b)	not easy to find or obtain
3	ration	c)	sourcing from a lot of different suppliers
4	withhold	d)	predicting future demand
5	run out (of)	e)	control the supply of something
6	scarce	f)	when products have sold so well that there are none left
7	alienate	g)	information given in advance about when something is happening
8	must-have products	h)	use up all of something
9	multi-sourcing	i)	products that everybody wants
10	notice	j)	deliberately keep something back

2 Find five words from Exercise 1 used for talking about product shortages.

3 Organise the words from Exercise 2 into three groups: nouns, verbs and adjectives.

4 Which word in Exercise 2 has the same meaning as *in short supply*?

B Sentence completion

Complete these sentences using words from Exercise A.

1 By creating the impression that 'must-have' products are .... , companies hope to increase interest and push up demand.

2 When launching new products, there is a suspicion that companies like Apple deliberately .... or even .... stock as a way of stimulating demand.

3 The risk of .... of stock is that customers will get frustrated and buy a competitor's product.

4 Product shortages can quickly result in empty shelves and complete ....-........ .

5 Because sales were higher than expected, the new LX40 was .... until production could be increased.

C Language of increase and decrease

1 Find words in the article with the same meaning to replace the words in italic in these guidelines.

   1 It's important that you are able to increase or *reduce*[a] production *quickly*[b], so make sure you negotiate flexible contracts.

   2 When choosing suppliers, make sure they are able to *increase*[a] deliveries to meet sudden *increases*[b] in demand.

   3 *Extending*[a] your supply base is also a good idea. It will enable you to *increase*[b] production *fast*[c] in different locations and use components from different sources.

2 Think of at least two other:

   1 nouns for expressing the idea of an increase or decrease.

   2 verbs for expressing the idea of increasing or decreasing something.

   3 adverbs for describing the rate or speed of change.

D Synonyms

1   Find adjectives in the article which mean the same as these words.

1   correct (paragraph B)
2   difficult (paragraph B)
3   advanced (paragraph C)
4   real (paragraph E)
5   nearer (paragraph G)
6   expensive (paragraph G)
7   exact (paragraph I)
8   shared (paragraph I)
9   quick to react (paragraph J)
10 unrestricted (paragraph J)

2   Find another noun in paragraph I which means *forecasts*.

E Prepositions

Complete these sentences using the prepositions in the box.

at	by	from	in	in	of	on	to	to	up	with

1   Forecasting demand correctly and getting products ....^{a} the right place ....^{b} the right time are challenges all companies face.

2   Manufacturers need sophisticated forecasting tools to predict unexpected increases ....^{a} demand, especially ....^{b} the period ....^{c} Christmas.

3   Make sure suppliers have the capacity to handle increased demand as part .... normal service.

4   Choose flexible suppliers, for example those who are able to increase deliveries ....^{a} 25 per cent, ...^{b} just a few week's notice.

5   Increase your supply base so that you buy components .... different sources.

6   Forecasting demand correctly depends .... having the right forecasting tools.

OVER TO YOU

1   Use information from the article and your own ideas to prepare a set of guidelines for minimising risks caused by temporary surges in demand.

2   Act out a meeting to negotiate prices with a supplier. You need them to be able to step up production at short notice.

3   Do you agree that running out of a well-publicised electronic gadget or a 'must-have' toy or game will damage a company and result in lost customers? Why? / Why not? Find examples to support your view.

This article looks at the operating and logistics strategies that have made the Spanish company Zara a top fashion retailer.

BEFORE YOU READ

Discuss these questions.

1 Talk about a successful fashion retail company in your country. What are the reasons for its success?
2 Have you ever shopped at Zara, H&M, Iniglow or Mango? Who are their stores aimed at? What makes them different from other fashion retailers?
3 In fashion retailing, what makes a supply chain effective, e.g. rapid turnaround of the latest looks, flexible suppliers, efficient and quick distribution to stores, etc.?

READING

A Understanding the main ideas

Read the article on the opposite page and say whether these statements are true (T) or false (F). Correct the false ones.

1 Zara has developed an innovative approach to fashion retailing.
2 Stock in its stores is constantly changing.
3 It doesn't source anything from outside Europe.
4 All manufacturing is carried out in Zara's own factories.
5 Products for all its markets go through its two distribution centres in Spain.
6 Zara has its own transport company to deliver merchandise to its stores.
7 It prefers its stores to have too much stock rather than too little stock.
8 Zara is an example of a very successful fast-fashion retailer.

B Understanding details

1 Read the article again and find information to complete this profile of Zara.

Target customers: ....[1]
HQ: La Coruña, Galicia (north-west Spain)
Main competitors: ...., ... and ....[2]
Business objectives: .... and ....[3]
Distribution centres: .... and ....[4]

Zara wins at fast fashion

A Successful Spanish company Zara produces and sells fashionable clothing. Its core customers are 18–35-year-old women. It offers them the latest fashions at affordable prices. To keep their interest, stock is constantly changed
5 and updated. New deliveries arrive on a twice-weekly basis. Few products are available in store for more than a month, adding a sense of exclusivity and pressure to buy.

B Zara competes directly with companies such as Gap, Mango and the Italian giant Benetton. All are examples
10 of companies that use quick-response logistics. Zara has achieved rapid growth and success in a highly competitive environment. This reflects its ability to implement an operating strategy based on dual objectives of minimising stock and responding quickly to market needs even more
15 effectively than its competitors.

C About 20 per cent of its merchandise – items with the widest and longest-lasting appeal – is imported as finished goods from low-cost manufacturing countries, mostly in Asia Pacific. The rest is produced by quick response.
20 Around 50 per cent of all merchandise is manufactured at the company's own factories and network of smaller contractors, situated near to its distribution centres in Galicia in the north-west of Spain. The rest is produced elsewhere in Spain or other European countries.

D Zara's manufacturing systems are similar in many ways to those developed so successfully by its competitor Benetton, but improved using ideas developed together with car manufacturer Toyota. Only those business activities that improve cost efficiency through economies of scale are
30 carried out in house (such as dyeing, cutting, labelling and packaging). All other manufacturing activities, including labour-intensive finishing, are done by small sub-contractors, each specialising in one particular part of the production process or garment type. These sub-contractors work
35 exclusively for Zara's parent, Inditex SA. In return, they receive any technological, financial and logistical support necessary to meet Zara's strict targets for time and quality.

Zara keeps inventory costs to a minimum because they only pay for the completed garments.

E Finished goods are sent to the company's two distribution centres in La Coruña and Zaragoza, where they are labelled, price-tagged (all items have international price tags with the price in relevant currencies) and packed. From there, they are carried by specialist contractors by road and/or air to
45 the stores. Road is used for journeys of 24 hours or less, while air freight is used for longer distances. All deliveries are completed within 48 hours.

F Stock allocations for the shops are calculated centrally, rather than in-store, because production is always kept at a
50 level slightly below expected sales to keep stock moving. True to its original objectives, the complete design, manufacturing and delivery cycle takes only four to five weeks, and the system is flexible enough to deal with any sudden changes in demand.

from *Logistics and Supply Chain Management – Creating Value-Adding Networks* by Martin Christopher

2 Complete this chart about Zara's manufacturing activities.

manufacturing/logistics activity	location
........[1] and dyeing	Zara's own factories
other manufacturing activities and finishing	........[2]
labelling, ...[3] and packaging	........[4]
stock allocation	commercial team at ....[5]
shipping to stores	........[6]

VOCABULARY

A Definitions

Match these words and phrases from the article (1–9) with their meanings (a–i).

1	exclusivity	a)	financial advantage gained from producing in large quantities and therefore selling more cheaply
2	quick-response logistics	b)	process of sharing stock, e.g. among a group of stores
3	economies of scale	c)	transport goods by air
4	contractors	d)	an item of clothing
5	labour-intensive	e)	when something desirable is limited in availability
6	garment	f)	labels on products which say how much they cost
7	price tags	g)	needing a lot of workers to do the work
8	air freight	h)	organisations working under contract to produce goods
9	stock allocations	i)	a strategy for reducing order lead times, increasing frequency of delivery and reducing average order size

B Word partnerships

1 Find words in the article that follow these nouns to form noun–noun partnerships.

    1 market
    2 manufacturing
    3 production
    4 inventory
    5 distribution
    6 design/manufacturing/delivery

2 Find three other noun–noun partnerships in Exercise A for talking about distribution.

C Sentence completion

Use word partnerships from Exercise B to complete these sentences.

1 Throughout the ...., there are regular inspections to make sure products meet the high standards.

2 Each shop receives new .... several times a week, based on its current sales and inventory levels.

3 For our European market, we use single ...., which show all the different prices by country.

4 The high turnover of products and our efficient distribution mean that we are able to keep .... low.

5 Every week, one million items are distributed to the stores through our two regional ....

6 The .... from warehouse to customer has been cut to three days by switching to air freight.

D Synonyms

Match each word from the article (1–7) with one which has a similar meaning (a–g).

1 core
2 implement
3 reacting
4 merchandise
5 exclusively
6 strict
7 a minimum

a) goods
b) the lowest amount possible
c) main
d) responding
e) tough and exacting
f) only
g) put into practice

E Passives

1 The writer uses the passive when describing Zara's operational processes. Complete these sentences.

1 About 20 per cent of its merchandise [...] .... as finished goods ... (lines 16–18)

2 All other manufacturing activities [...] .... small sub-contractors ... (lines 31–32)

2 Read paragraphs E and F again carefully and find at least four other examples of the passive.

3 Complete these sentences using the passive form of the verbs in the box.

attach   cut   dye   give   source

1 Suppliers .... about two weeks to move from design to production of a new item.

2 Today, nearly 65 per cent of production .... in Europe.

3 Near Zara's distribution centre in La Coruña, fabric .... and .... by robots in highly automated factories.

4 Security and price tags .... to each item before shipping to the stores.

F Prepositions

Match the sentence halves to make sentences about Zara's activities and distribution.

1 New deliveries arrive
2 Zara competes directly
3 Zara keeps inventory costs
4 All deliveries are completed

a) **within** 48 hours.
b) **on** a twice-weekly basis.
c) **with** companies such as Gap and Mango.
d) **to** a minimum.

OVER TO YOU

1 In what ways are Zara's operating strategies different to those of its competitors? Make notes for a presentation about: sourcing, manufacturing, distribution and transportation, stock allocation and replenishment.

2 Choose a company. Then prepare a diagram and commentary to explain how it distributes stock to its customers. Include the passive where it fits.

3 What are the potential risks for Zara of distributing products for all its global markets through its two distribution centres in the north-west of Spain?

4 How applicable are the principles of quick-response logistics to other sectors and industries?

Using RFID for managing stock

This unit looks at the developments in the use of RFID (radio frequency identification) at Metro AG, the German retailer.

1 Match the photos in the article (1–3) with the correct description (a–c).

   a) barcode
   b) RFID tag
   c) moving pallets in a warehouse

2 Think of three applications of RFID technology in:

   a) everyday life
   b) warehousing and distribution.

3 What are the benefits of RFID for managing inventories in retailing?

4 What are the chances of RFID totally replacing barcode technology?

READING

A **Understanding the main points**

Read the article on the opposite page and choose the best option to complete each statement.

1 RFID is *already* / *not yet* technically reliable enough to replace barcodes.

2 Metro has moved *totally* / *partially* to using RFID throughout its supply chain.

3 At the time of writing the article, Metro was using RFID to track *pallets only* / *pallets and cases of products*.

4 The main motivation for Metro's move to RFID is to *reduce operating costs* / *improve customers' shopping experience*.

5 The high cost of RFID tags makes it unlikely that Metro will use the technology throughout its supply chain *ever* / *for many years*.

6 Metro *invests a lot* / *doesn't invest much* in developing new applications for RFID.

B **Understanding details**

1 Read the article again. What do these numbers and dates refer to?

   a) March 2004   e) €0.01
   b) 25   f) 2003
   c) 40 (x2)   g) 20
   d) 2,300

RFID – the price must be right

by John Blau

A A shopper takes a bottle of shampoo from the supermarket shelf, and a signal from a state-of-the-art smart tag is sent to staff, updating them on stock levels. RFID – short for radio frequency identification, a technology that uses radio waves to automatically identify objects – is now working well and ready to replace conventional bar codes.

B German retailer Metro AG, the world's fifth-largest retailer, has been introducing RFID in stages along its supply chain since March 2004. So far, it has 25 distribution centres using the technology, mostly on the wooden pallets which carry the goods; more than 40 suppliers now attach RFID tags to their pallets. Recently, it has also started using tags on individual cases of products.

C The ultimate aim is to use RFID at all levels, including the individual item, at all of its 2,300 locations – but that will not happen for years, according to Gerd Wolfram, Managing Director of MGI, Metro Group Information Technology.

D 'We will see RFID increasingly replace bar codes for certain products, but the technology won't be used to identify all products for at least 15 years,' he says, giving high unit prices for the tags as one of the main reasons. Unit prices, Wolfram says, will need to drop to €0.01 per tag or less to make RFID a viable alternative to a bar code.

E Metro sees RFID technology as a way to manage the huge flow of merchandise in and out of stores more effectively, while at the same time enabling the company to reduce inventory losses and labour costs. Wolfram says: 'We firmly believe that we'll able to lower our operating costs with this technology and in time provide

our customers with a better shopping experience.'

F Since 2003, Metro has been testing RFID in a real retail situation at the Extra supermarket in Rheinberg, near Düsseldorf, as part of its Future Store Initiative. Among the innovative RFID applications that Metro is currently testing at the store is the 'smart-shelf', which automatically informs staff when to replenish merchandise. RFID tags are attached to packages of Gillette razor blades or plastic bottles of shampoo from Procter & Gamble. As customers pick up the tagged products, signals are sent electronically to the merchandise management system, which tracks the number in stock and sends out an alert to staff carrying PDAs (personal digital assistants) to tell them when shelves need restocking.

G Metro is also carrying out development work on RFID at its RFID Innovation Centre in nearby Neuss, where it is testing more than 40 applications. The focus of most of these applications is logistics, warehousing and retail operations, but a few also involve consumers. For instance, they are developing a 'smart fridge' which identifies products and informs household members when expiry dates are coming up.

H At Neuss, Metro is also collaborating with around 20 technology partners, including key IT industry companies IBM, Intel and SAP to develop the technology further.

---

2 **Read paragraphs F and G again and answer these questions.**

1 What happens at these Metro locations?

a) the Extra supermarket in Rheinberg   b) Neuss

2 Metro is testing these two new applications: a 'smart shelf' and a 'smart fridge'.

a) How will the 'smart shelf' help staff in Metro's retail stores?

b) How will the 'smart fridge' help consumers?

VOCABULARY

A Definitions

Match these words and phrases from the article (1–7) with their meanings (a–g).

1	smart	a)	an advance warning that something is going to happen
2	pallets	b)	controlled precisely, through the use of computer technology
3	applications	c)	the date on which something can no longer be used or is no longer safe to eat
4	alert	d)	all the people living in one home
5	PDA	e)	flat wooden or metal surfaces for moving or storing heavy goods
6	household members	f)	particular uses that something has
7	expiry date	g)	short for 'personal digital assistant'; a very small computer for storing information, often with a touch screen

B Word partnerships

Find words in the article that follow these nouns to make noun–noun partnerships.

1 RFID
2 inventory
3 innovation
4 shopping
5 logistics/warehousing/retail
6 technology

C Sentence completion

Use word partnerships from Exercise B to complete these sentences.

1 R....... t........^{a} has been around since the 1970s, but so far has been too expensive to replace barcodes for all l....... o........^{b} in retail.

2 One strong argument for using R....... t........^{a} on pallets and cases is to reduce i........ l........^{b}.

3 At their i........ c........^{a}, Metro is working on new R....... a........^{b} that will make their r........ o........^{c} more effective and also improve customers' s........ e........^{d}.

D Vocabulary development

Decide which verb does *not* go with the nouns or noun phrases in bold.

1	replenish / restock / refill	**merchandise**
2	fall / reduce / lower	**inventory costs / operating costs**
3	test / experiment / try out	**RFID applications**
4	track / trace / follow	**stock**
5	collaborate with / work together with / act with	**technology partners**
6	introduce / grow / develop	**new RFID applications**
7	attach / join / fix	**RFID tags**
8	carry out / do / make	**development work / research**

E **Word search**

Find adjectives in the article which fit these meanings.

1 high-tech and modern (paragraph A)
2 traditional (paragraph A)
3 final (paragraph C)
4 single (paragraph C)
5 a number of (paragraph D)
6 workable (paragraph D)
7 very big (paragraph E)
8 new and original (paragraph F)

F **Prepositions**

Use the prepositions in the box to complete these sentences.

at for in in of on out since to to with

1 Metro has been introducing RFID technology ....[a] stages ....[b] 2003.
2 RFID tags are now attached ....[a] pallets and also used ....[b] individual cases of products.
3 The price ....[a] tags is still too high to make them a real alternative ....[b] bar codes.
4 Metro is collaborating ....[a] IT technology partners to develop new applications ....[b] logistics, warehousing and retail operations.
5 Metro carries ....[a] most of its RFID development work ....[b] its Innovation Centre ....[c] Neuss.

OVER TO YOU

1 Research some current and potential RFID applications in one of these sectors (or a sector of your choice). Then present your findings.
  - manufacturing, e.g. tracking work in progress
  - retail, e.g. reducing stock-outs
  - distribution and logistics, e.g. reducing lost inventory
2 What are the benefits and limitations of barcode and RFID technology for logistics, warehousing and retail operations? Prepare a short report summarising the case for one of them.
3 Discuss how RFID could help this company.

> Montomar produces flash memory cards and drives for electronics retailers. Its warehouse operators need to be able track shipments to their main customer's two distribution centres more efficiently. Orders from this customer fluctuate, but they need to be able to handle up to a 100 orders a day, with shipments of up to 250,000 items. Merchandise is taking too long to leave the warehouse – the target is two to four days. Mistakes also happen during the boxing and loading of orders onto pallets.

63

Reducing a company's carbon footprint

This unit describes how Jaguar Land Rover (JLR) reduced the carbon emissions in its supply chain.

BEFORE YOU READ

Discuss these questions.

1 How would you define the term *carbon footprint*?
2 What aspects of its supply chain do you think Jaguar Land Rover focused on to reduce carbon emissions?
3 In what ways can transport by ship be made more carbon efficient?

READING

A **Understanding the main points**

Read the article on the opposite page and answer these questions.

1 How has Jaguar Land Rover changed its environmental approach since 2003?
2 What is JLR's integrated Europe-wide supply chain?
3 How has JLR reduced emissions in its transport of goods by ship?

B **Understanding details**

Read the article again and answer these questions.

1 When did Jaguar Land Rover begin its campaign to reduce its carbon footprint?
2 What was the carbon footprint of JLR's total supply chain at the start of 2008?
3 What is their target 10 years from the date of the article?
4 Who owns JLR?
5 At the time of the article, how many vehicles did JLR produce per year in the UK?
6 What was JLR's original aim when it set up its integrated Europe-wide supply chain?
7 How successful has this been in reducing CO_2 emissions?
8 How does JLR plan to reduce carbon emissions further in its integrated Europe-wide supply chain?
9 What is the difference between the purchase price and the total landed cost of materials purchased from suppliers?
10 In what other way has JLR managed to reduce the number of road miles in its transportation of vehicles?
11 What extra effort has JLR made to reduce emissions in its ship transportation?
12 What is the Orcelle project?

How Jaguar Land Rover reduced its carbon footprint

by Rod Newing

A In 2003, Jaguar Land Rover did not know the carbon footprint of its supply chain. Now, it has been measured, reduction targets have been set, measures are being taken, and the results are being monitored.

B 'Our total supply-chain carbon footprint in January 2008 was 186,076 tonnes a year,' says Kevin Wall, the company's Material, Planning and Logistics Director. 'We are on target to reduce this by more than 2,000 tonnes year on year and we have a 10-year plan to eliminate 90m road miles.'

C Jaguar Cars is one of the world's premier makers of luxury cars, and Land Rover's four-wheel drive vehicles are world famous. Together, the two companies, which were acquired by Tata Motors from Ford Motor in 2008, manufacture 290,000 vehicles a year in the UK.

D In 2003, Jaguar Land Rover set up an integrated Europe-wide supply chain to collect components from 380 suppliers based in the UK and Europe. The aim was to maximise the full capacity of a trailer by consolidating five or six suppliers in a similar geographical area. This has reduced average road miles per week from 59,280 to 30,780, a 52-per-cent saving.

E Although created to reduce costs, it has also eliminated CO_2 emissions of 1,772 tonnes a year. The third-party logistics contract has just been rebid, and next-generation truck engines were specified, to reduce emissions and improve economy by 10–12 per cent.

F 'Ten years ago, our supplier base was mainly in the UK, but now it is truly global,' says Mr Wall. 'You can't look at the purchase price any more, you have to look at the total landed cost, including freight, packaging, customs and the cost of returning any unique containers. It is difficult to calculate, but we have used this basis for

several years, and it takes into account both the financial and environmental implications of global sourcing.'

G The company has been trying to switch vehicle delivery from road to trains. Finished vehicles for the US, Australia and Japan go to Southampton by rail. This has eliminated 777,925 road miles a year, equating to 1,188 tonnes of CO_2.

H From Southampton, vehicles are transported by Wallenius Wilhelmsen ships. In partnership, the two organisations have optimised fleet utilisation, streamlined routes and run vessels – where possible – at more economical speeds. Most significantly, instead of normal bunker fuel, the company pays extra for the ships to use low-sulphur fuel, which contains 1.3 per cent of the mineral, compared with an International Maritime Organisation target of

4.5 per cent. Between 2001 and 2007, this low-sulphur fuel saved 98,500 tonnes of sulphur dioxide emissions, a reduction of 43 per cent, and has cut CO_2 emissions by 17 per cent.

I Future projects include reviewing vessel steaming speeds. A two-knot reduction saves 244kg of CO_2 per transported unit, 21 per cent less than present.

J JLR is also exploring Wallenius Wilhelmsen's Orcelle project for a lightweight, environmentally sound ship that can carry 10,000 cars. Using solar, wind and wave power, it does not release any emissions into the atmosphere or the ocean.

VOCABULARY

A   Definitions

Find words and phrases in the article which match these meanings.

1   are likely to reach the result they are aiming for (paragraph B)
2   planned and implemented a new system (paragraph D)
3   explained in an exact and detailed way (paragraph E)
4   possible results of a plan or an action (paragraph F)
5   improved to make simpler or more efficient (paragraph H)
6   examining something to decide if changes need to be made (paragraph I)
7   weighing very little (paragraph J)
8   good for the environment (paragraph J)

B   Sentence completion

Use words and phrases from Exercise A in the correct form to complete these sentences.

1   A few years ago, JLR .... an integrated Europe-wide supply chain.
2   Global sourcing has financial and environmental .... which were not considered when the process first started.
3   In order to reduce fuel consumption, JLR is .... the speed at which ships travel when transporting its cars.
4   One aim of the Orcelle project is to build .... ships which will need much less power than heavier, conventional ships.
5   JLR .... to reduce its supply-chain carbon footprint by more than 2,000 tonnes, year on year.
6   Ships of the future will need to be .... so that they produce very low or even no emissions.
7   When JLR requested new bids for its logistics contract, it .... next-generation truck engines to reduce emissions.
8   Another way to reduce emissions and fuel consumption is to .... and shorten routes for trucks and ships.

C   Prepositions to express figures

Complete these extracts using *between*, *by*, *from*, *per* or *to*. Some can be used more than once.

1   We are on target to reduce our carbon footprint .... more than 2,000 tonnes year on year.
2   JLR's integrated Europe-wide supply chain has reduced average road miles ....[a] week ....[b] 59,280 ....[c] 30,780, a 52-per-cent saving.
3   Using next-generation truck engines will improve economy .... 10–12 per cent.
4   Switching from road to rail has eliminated 777,925 road miles a year, equating .... 1,188 tonnes of CO_2.
5   ....[a] 2001 and 2007, the use of low-sulphur fuel cut CO_2 emissions ....[b] 17 per cent.
6   A two-knot reduction in vessel steaming speeds saves 244kg of CO_2 .... transported unit.

D Word partnerships

Match these words to make noun–noun partnerships from the article.

1	carbon	a)	contract
2	road	b)	price
3	logistics	c)	delivery
4	supplier	d)	miles
5	purchase	e)	utilisation
6	vehicle	f)	footprint
7	fleet	g)	base

E Sentence completion

Use the word partnerships from Exercise D to complete these sentences.

1   JLR has just organised a rebid of its .... for transportation of parts and materials.

2   Over the last five or six years, JLR has substantially reduced the number of .... used in the transport of its parts and finished vehicles.

3   One way that JLR and Wallenius Wilhelmsen have reduced the carbon emissions in ship transport is by optimising ....

4   As a result of all its efforts, JLR's .... has been significantly reduced.

5   JLR's .... , from which it purchases components, used to be mainly in the UK, but now it is global.

6   To assess both the financial and environmental implications of global sourcing, JLR takes into account the total landed cost of its materials rather than just the ....

7   To reduce its carbon emissions, JLR has switched as much of its .... as possible from road to rail.

F Word search

1   Find four verbs in the article which give the idea of improvement.

2   Find three verbs with the meaning of *to lower* or *to stop completely*.

OVER TO YOU

1   Imagine you are a transport and logistics consultant brought in by a car manufacturer to advise it on how to reduce the carbon footprint of its supply chain. Use the ideas and figures in the article as the basis to prepare and deliver a presentation of your recommendations to the board of the company.

2   Look for details about Wallenius Wilhelmsen's Orcelle project on the Internet. Then discuss whether this concept will be the cargo ship of the future or just a nice, but impractical idea. Give reasons to support your arguments.

Moving beyond logistics

This article considers how companies can become more energy efficient and improve their environmental performance.

Discuss these questions.

1 The most obvious way for companies to be more environmentally friendly in how they operate their supply chains is by looking for efficiencies in their transport and logistics systems. Give some examples of what they could do.

2 In what other ways can companies make their supply chains more environmentally friendly?

3 In what ways do you think improvements in packaging design can make a company's operations more environmentally friendly?

READING

A Understanding the main points

Read the article on the opposite page and choose the statement that expresses the main idea in the article most accurately.

a) Companies should put their main environmental efforts into making their transport and logistics as efficient as possible.

b) Moving goods by sea is more environmentally friendly than transporting them by road.

c) Companies should look at how they can be more energy efficient in every part of their supply chain.

B Understanding details

Read the article again and answer these questions.

1 What part of a company's supply chain is a particularly significant contributor to climate change?

2 At what stages in the supply chain can companies start looking at ways of improving sustainability?

3 What example is given of inefficiencies in the transportation of goods?

4 What is considered the most carbon-efficient form of transport?

5 In what ways, apart from transport, can companies look for efficiency and cost savings in their supply chain?

6 Why are mergers often bad for supply-chain efficiency?

7 What parts of their supply chains are progressive companies looking at?

8 What two examples are given of where environmental improvements can be made during a product's lifecycle?

9 In what ways can changes in packaging design produce environmental improvements?

Green supply chains: moving beyond logistics

by Sarah Murray

A As companies start to examine the environmental footprint of their supply chains, attention has often focused on transport and logistics. But while the movement of products across the globe is one of the most visible signs of the contribution of supply chains to climate change, many organisations are starting to look for efficiencies throughout their operations, taking decisions on sustainability back as far as the design stage.

B Of course, with rising fuel costs, the argument for addressing transport issues is a compelling one. And there is plenty of room to iron out inefficiencies in long-distance cargo haulage. 'In Europe, typically 25 to 30 per cent of vehicles are running around empty. That's because we're not optimising the backhauls or because vehicles are ending up in the wrong place,' says Jonathan Wright, of the supply-chain practice at Accenture.

C Some forms of transport are more energy efficient than others. Using ships is generally seen as the most carbon-efficient means of freight transportation, for example. Companies are exploring the idea of putting some products on barges, while others argue that countries with canal systems, such as the UK, should put them back into commercial use.

D However, Jayashankar Swaminathan, of the University of North Carolina's Kenan-Flagler Business School, points out that the configuration side of the supply chain – that is, where products are being made and stored – also drives efficiency. 'It's about where you have the warehouses, suppliers and manufacturing facilities,' he says. 'If you want your supply chain to have minimum cost but also minimum effect environmentally, you have to go back and revisit those things.'

E Part of the problem lies in the consolidation of many industries. When companies merge with or buy other companies, they may find that warehouses and transport networks are no longer in appropriate positions for the new business, generating more truck movements than necessary. 'Companies may find they have a warehouse on one side of a European border and one on the other side. It takes a long time and it's quite complex to merge those two supply chains and work out that you need one big warehouse and three satellite warehouses,' says Jonathan Wright.

F But while the logistics side of global supply chains provides many areas in which companies become more efficient and sustainable, organisations are also starting to look more broadly across the chain for environmental improvements. According to Omer Abdullah of the Smart Cube, a London- and Chicago-based consultancy, progressive companies are looking at the full lifecycle of their entire supply chain, assessing the environmental impact at each stage, both of energy and materials.

G This takes companies all the way back to the design stage of their operations, where they can reduce or eliminate toxic chemicals or make the product easier to take apart at the recycling stage. Packaging design also has an impact. Better designs help not only cut down on materials used but also reduce transport-related emissions because more items fit into each container.

VOCABULARY

A Understanding expressions

Choose the best explanation for each phrase from the article.

1 '... examine *the environmental footprint of their supply chains* ...' (lines 1–3)
   a) the degree to which their supply chains are environmentally friendly
   b) the impact their supply chains have on the environment

2 '... *taking decisions on sustainability back as far as the design stage*.' (lines 10–12)
   a) looking at how they can design products to make them more environmentally friendly
   b) postponing decisions at the design stage until they are sure they are environmentally friendly

3 '... *the argument for addressing transport issues is a compelling one*.' (lines 13–15)
   a) companies now have an obligation to consider the environmental impact of their transport systems
   b) there are strong reasons to improve the environmental impact of their transport systems

4 '... there is *plenty of room to iron out inefficiencies in long-distance cargo haulage*.' (lines 15–17)
   a) long-distance transport is not very energy efficient
   b) long-distance transport can certainly become more energy efficient

5 '... we're not *optimising the backhauls* ...' (lines 20–21)
   a) making effective use of trucks which return from a delivery empty
   b) improving the delivery schedules of truck fleets

6 '... *the configuration side of the supply chain* [...] *also drives efficiency*.' (lines 38–41)
   a) the efficiency of supply chains also depends on how products are designed
   b) the way the supply chain is structured and organised is also important for efficiency

7 '*Part of the problem lies in the consolidation of many industries*.' (lines 48–49)
   a) mergers and acquisitions are partly to blame for inefficiencies in supply chains
   b) when companies merge, they can achieve economies of scale in their supply chain

8 '... starting to *look more broadly across the chain for environmental improvements*.' (lines 68–70)
   a) look at all parts of the supply chain to see if improvements can be made
   b) compare their supply chain with that of other companies to see what they can learn

B Verbs and prepositions

Match the verbs (1–11) with the prepositions (a–k) to form phrasal verbs from the article.

1	point	a)	back
2	put	b)	down on
3	look	c)	out
4	focus	d)	out
5	run	e)	up
6	iron	f)	back
7	cut	g)	apart
8	go	h)	for
9	end	i)	around
10	take	j)	on
11	work	k)	out

C **Sentence completion**

Use the phrasal verbs from Exercise B in the correct form to complete these sentences.

1 When companies think about reducing their environmental footprint, they usually .... transport and logistics first.

2 There are plenty of ways to .... inefficiencies in long-distance transportation of goods.

3 Many trucks .... empty because they have no load when they return to the depot.

4 In other cases, due to bad planning, trucks .... in the wrong place.

5 After a merger, companies need time to .... how many warehouses they need.

6 Supply-chain experts have .... that there are other ways to reduce the environmental impact of a supply chain than just concentrating on transport and logistics.

7 Some people believe that canal systems should be .... into use for commercial purposes.

8 Many organisations are starting to .... ways of improving efficiencies at all stages in their supply chain.

9 If companies want to make efficiencies across their entire supply chain, they need to .... and look at how their products are made and stored, as well as how they are transported.

10 Part of the environmental impact of a product is how easy it is to .... for recycling at the end of its life.

11 New designs in packaging will enable producers to .... the amount of materials used.

D **Word development**

Many adjectives in English form the negative by adding a prefix at the start of the positive form of the word, e.g. *efficient – inefficient*.

Add the correct prefix (*in–*, *ir–* or *un–*) to form the negative of these adjectives used in the article.

1 appropriate   3 relevant   5 necessary

2 sustainable   4 visible   6 progressive

OVER TO YOU

There is a big debate in the automotive industry about the best way to reduce fuel consumption and carbon emissions.

Japanese car manufacturers, especially Toyota with its Prius model, have opted for hybrid vehicles – a combination of electric motor and conventional petrol engine. In urban areas, the car uses a combination of battery and engine power, and the petrol engine takes over at higher speeds or when the battery is low. But hybrid vehicles are heavier and more expensive to produce than conventional engine cars. Moreover, the battery may need to be changed after a number of years, and is expensive to recycle.

Most of the European car makers, especially in Germany, have opted for a conventional diesel engine specially designed to be highly fuel efficient and low on emissions, using new technologies such as stop-start. They combine this with using lightweight materials when building the car, fitting low-profile tyres, etc. These cars use more environmentally friendly materials that can be more easily recycled at the end of the car's life.

Discuss which approach you think is better and give your reasons. What kind of car would you buy?

This unit considers the ways that manufacturers can be environmentally sensitive at every stage in their supply chain.

BEFORE YOU READ

Discuss these questions.

1 Companies are increasingly expected to meet the ethical expectations of their customers in the ways they do business. Give some examples of these ethical expectations.

2 What are typical problems that companies can have with their suppliers about issues of environmental responsibility?

3 In what ways can companies try to ensure that their suppliers operate in an environmentally sensitive way?

READING

A Understanding the main points

Read the article on the opposite page and answer these questions.

1 Who is putting the main pressure on companies to be environmentally sensitive?
2 What is the role of suppliers in the environmental process?
3 Why is it difficult to check environmental practices in areas such as Shenzen in China?
4 What will the benefit be for those companies that can successfully prove they are environmentally responsible?

B Understanding details

Read the article again and say whether these statements are true (T), false (F) or there is not enough information given (N). Identify the part of the article that gives this information.

1 Government regulations are the main reason that companies try to be environmentally sensitive.
2 Customers also expect companies to be environmentally sensitive.
3 Companies only focus on environmental issues if they are forced to by government regulations.
4 Apple's first version of its iPhone contained dangerous chemicals.
5 The focus on environmental responsibility needs to go all the way along the supply chain.
6 Hewlett-Packard is the leader in monitoring its global suppliers for health and safety.
7 HP has at least 60 suppliers in China.
8 HP is convinced that bribery and corruption are big problems in emerging markets.
9 HP does not feel it can fully rely on health and safety regulations in countries such as China.
10 Computer manufacturers pay little attention to environmental issues in their supply chains.

Demand spreads along the supply chain

by Dan Ilett

A Large international companies are used to dealing with compliance regulations – someone publishes a new rule, the company obeys, ticks a box and moves on to the next. But they now face the problem of meeting the ethical expectations of customers as well. Part of this means showing the world they have environmentally friendly credentials, which is not so easy to prove.

B According to Gareth Pickles, of environmental consultant Delta-Simons Shining Earth, 'there's been a shift from the government driving this, to the customer. Consumers are looking to businesses to improve their environmental credentials.'

C While eco-campaigners have criticised drivers of large vehicles for some years, the spotlight is turning towards companies and their technology. For example, Greenpeace criticised Apple's first iPhone when it was launched, claiming it contained hazardous chemicals.

D This means companies have to look harder at the technology they use – not only at energy consumption but at the manufacture of components – and that means choosing suppliers that can also prove the environmental credentials of their suppliers. Hewlett-Packard, for example, claims it has audited its top suppliers around the world on health and environment.

E Bonnie Nixon-Gardiner is the Global Manager for HP's supply chain and environmental programme. On her way to China to test how green 60 of the company's suppliers really are, she says: 'People were asking: "are you aware of the mining and extraction practices of metals you use?" The industry said it could not possibly influence the sourcing of that, but we weren't happy with that answer, so we've been trying to find out whether our suppliers know where they're sourcing from.' She says: 'Many laws do exist in emerging markets, but it's a matter of inspecting them. Maybe there is corruption or bribery. If you take a place like Shenzhen in China, there are 1.5m residents but 9m immigrant workers. The infrastructure isn't there to deal with that many factories, so we have our own health and safety officers.

F 'For example, it's not good enough when a company comes in and picks up chemicals for disposal. We really try to make sure no one dumps them somewhere,' adds Ms Nixon-Gardiner. The demand for greener credentials is here to stay: 'It makes good business sense to do it.'

G IT vendors seem to realise the importance of at least talking the green talk. And many have tried to set environmental standards that all component suppliers around the world have to respect. For example, Dell, Intel, Apple, HP, Sun and others have signed up to the Electronic Industry Code of Conduct, an initiative to improve conditions in the electronics supply chain, especially in countries such as China, where much equipment is made.

H A report from analyst Gartner adds: 'Vendors that achieve this – get their timing right, and exploit the opportunities that an environmentally sensitised market and supply chain will present – are likely to become more successful in the market.'

FT

VOCABULARY

A Definitions

Match these words from the article (1–10) with their meanings (a–j).

1	compliance	a)	dangerous
2	credentials	b)	a new plan to solve a particular problem
3	driving	c)	process of removing minerals from under the ground
4	criticised	d)	evidence that you can do what you say you can do
5	spotlight	e)	gets rid of something in an illegal way
6	hazardous	f)	when people obey a rule or law
7	extraction	g)	focus of attention
8	disposal	h)	when you get rid of something
9	dumps	i)	made negative comments about someone or something
10	initiative	j)	being the power behind something

B Verbs and prepositions

Complete these verbs and verb phrases using the prepositions in the box.

at   of   out   to   to   to   towards   up   up   with

1	to be used	5	to find ....
2	to look .... /	6	to deal ....
3	to turn	7	to pick ....
4	to be aware	8	to sign ....

C Vocabulary development

Replace the words in italic with verbs + prepositions from Exercise B. In one case, you will need to change the word order slightly.

1 When a company *collects* chemicals for disposal, it is important that they are not just dumped.

2 Consumers *expect* companies to improve their environmental credentials.

3 Most of the big international IT manufacturers have *agreed to follow* a code of conduct about how they source their components.

4 Many companies *are accustomed to* dealing with compliance regulations.

5 An important task for companies is to *discover* where their suppliers are sourcing their materials from.

6 In many emerging countries, the local authorities are not equipped to *handle* the full range of health and safety issues.

7 For many years, environmental concerns have focused on emissions caused by road transport, but now attention *is being directed at* the manufacturing process itself.

8 It is important for companies to *know* what processes their suppliers use when producing components.

9 In order to be fully environmentally sensitive, companies need to *examine* carefully the technology they use both in transportation and manufacturing.

D Word families

1 **What nouns can be formed from these verbs?**

1	source	6	exploit
2	publish	7	audit
3	improve	8	inspect
4	criticise	9	achieve
5	choose	10	prove

2 **What verbs can be formed from these nouns? In two cases, a preposition needs to be added.**

1	compliance	5	disposal
2	consumption	6	expectation
3	corruption	7	regulation
4	bribery	8	initiative

E Sentence completion

Use nouns and verbs from the answers to Exercise D in the correct form to complete these sentences.

1 Companies need to .... government regulations or they risk being fined.

2 An .... is a person who checks various processes both in their own company and in suppliers.

3 In recent years, there has been a big .... in the way companies have established their environmental credentials.

4 If companies use hazardous materials in their products, it is important that these .... correctly, rather than just being dumped.

5 Transporting goods by road .... a lot of energy.

6 When companies do environmental audits of their suppliers, they are looking for .... that they are operating in an environmentally sensitive way.

7 Customers of large companies .... them to carry out their business in an ethical and environmentally sensitive way.

OVER TO YOU

1 As an environmental auditor of suppliers of components, what aspects of the supplier's business will you inspect?

2 List all the questions you would ask a supplier to check that they are working in compliance with health and safety regulations and with environmental issues. Then role-play a visit to a supplier's factory where you meet the Head of Quality Systems.

3 You have discovered that one of your suppliers is not following correct environmental procedures. Hold a meeting with them to explain the problem and what they need to do if they wish to remain on your list of suppliers.

Check Test 1 (Units 1–9)

A **Use words and phrases from Units 1–9 to complete these sentences.**

1 C........ are parts which are built into the final product.

2 The company announced that it would close eight w........ and cut 600 jobs as it replaced smaller distribution centres with a network of larger ones.

3 Introducing c........-c........ measures can bring immediate savings and ensure that companies remain competitive in the longer term.

4 By reducing unnecessary i........, a company can minimise the need for warehousing space and handling.

5 If too much w........ c........ is tied up in stock, the company won't have the money it needs to develop the business.

6 A fast way to improve b........-l........ performance is to develop more efficient manufacturing techniques that reduce waste and the need for replacements.

7 The central aim of s........-c........ m........ is to have the right products in the right quantities (at the right place) at the right moment at minimal cost.

8 For retailers, delays in the supply chain can result in empty shelves and s........-o......... .

9 Having a highly effective supply chain increasingly gives a company a c........ e........ over its main rivals.

10 Manufacturers need to plan ahead and have accurate systems for estimating d........ for their products.

11 'F........-t........ supplier' is a common term for main supplier, especially in the automotive and computer industries.

12 Three tough years have forced TLM to reduce its s........ b........ from 2,000 suppliers to 900 today.

13 S........ s........ is when a company places all its purchasing needs with one supplier, often with the aim of negotiating better conditions.

14 Companies need to hold b........ s........ in order to maintain supplies when there are breakdowns in the production process or late deliveries from suppliers.

15 After implementing j........-i........-t........ methods to production and supply, the company managed to reduce production costs by 40 per cent and inventory costs by 30 per cent.

16 Developing and maintaining effective r........ with suppliers is hard work, especially when suppliers are located in different parts of the world.

17 A large order of customised parts may have a l........ t........ (order to delivery) of several weeks.

18 For many companies, a key motivation for o........ all or part of their operations is to reduce costs.

19 One big decision for DB Enterprises was whether to keep warehousing operations i........-h........ or to contract them out to a specialist company.

20 Most companies have a c........ o........ c........ which gives minimum standards for working conditions in their supplier factories.

B **Choose the best word or phrase to complete each of these sentences.**

1 To limit the risk of .... to supplies, it is important to assess the financial health of supply companies, for example their turnover and company results.

   a) disruption   b) disturbances   c) trouble   d) pitfalls

2 According to the terms of the contract, suppliers must pay a .... for late deliveries.

   a) fine   b) price   c) punishment   d) penalty

3 It is in every company's interest to keep .... levels at a minimum.

   a) customer satisfaction   b) inventory   c) production   d) delivery

4   The company has invested in new software for tracking every stage of order .... and billing.

   a) fulfilment   b) implementation   c) replenishment   d) replacement

5   Due mainly to high labour costs in the US, there has been a .... in production of clothing to low-cost developing countries.

   a) change   b) shift   c) movement   d) modification

6   Having more than one supplier for critical components can reduce the risk to a company's business if a supplier goes ....

   a) failed   b) insolvent   c) in debt   d) bankrupt

7   In difficult economic times, there is higher chance of companies ....

   a) failing   b) going wrong   c) withdrawing   d) breaking down

8   Product .... have a significant cost impact for companies – some of the most obvious being money, time, resources and lost reputation.

   a) innovations   b) shortages   c) inaccuracies   d) defects

9   The late arrival of critical components can result in .... delays throughout the production process.

   a) extra   b) knock-on   c) indirect   d) secondary

10   Energy costs .... an increasing percentage of total production costs for manufacturers across many sectors.

   a) account for   b) make   c) produce   d) justify

11   Late delivery of essential components meant we could not meet production targets and has led to production .... of 30 per cent for the last two months.

   a) restrictions   b) losses   c) shortfalls   d) shortages

12   If your sales .... are lower than the actual demand for a product, there is a risk of product shortages.

   a) results   b) forecasts   c) performance   d) requirements

13   Critical components for vehicles are manufactured by suppliers according to the manufacturer's design ....

   a) plan   b) conditions   c) specifications   d) instructions

14   At critical points during the production process, the buyer will want to carry out .... at the supplier's factory to check the quality.

   a) examinations   b) evaluations   c) investigations   d) inspections

15   .... reduces the risk of being dependent on a single supplier, but managing a lot of suppliers needs additional time and resources.

   a) Single-sourcing   b) Dual-sourcing   c) Multiple-sourcing   d) Exclusive

16   Low-cost labour encouraged many multinationals to .... their manufacturing operations to south-east Asia.

   a) subcontract   b) offshore   c) backshore   d) outsource

17   Despite rising costs and wage inflation, China still remains the top location for manufacturing ....

   a) investment   b) capacity   c) expenses   d) innovation

18   Maintaining .... standards has become an increasing challenge for large clothing retailers because of the size and complexity of supply chains.

   a) moral   b) honest   c) realistic   d) ethical

19   .... in the press about poor conditions in supplier factories abroad can damage a company's reputation with consumers and negatively affect its sales.

   a) Allegations   b) Statements   c) Worries   d) Suspicions

20   Labour costs in Vietnam are amongst the lowest in the world, but many garment workers are not paid a(n) .... wage (i.e. enough to cover basic costs of rent, food and bills).

   a) live   b) living   c) average   d) regular

Check Test 2 (Units 10–18)

A **Use words and phrases from Units 10–18 to complete these sentences.**

1 P........ produce, such as fresh fruit and vegetables, needs to be transported under special conditions.

2 Refrigerated c........ are used to transport fresh fruit and vegetables.

3 High-value produce, such as soft fruit, is a........-f........ rather than being transported by ship.

4 Food products cannot be displayed in a store after their s........-b........ d.........

5 With higher energy prices, the cost of t........ goods has increased a lot.

6 To reduce delivery costs, manufacturers are building p........ s........ closer to their customers.

7 Most companies are trying to reduce their c........ f........ because of increased concern about environmental issues.

8 Reduction in carbon e........ can be achieved by using sea and rail rather than road and air for the transport of goods.

9 R........ c........ is the result of too many vehicles being on the road at the same time.

10 E........ r........ is when a truck returns from a delivery without a load.

11 Evenings and weekends are o........-p........ times for delivering goods to stores.

12 The worst thing to happen to a retailer is to r........ o........ of a popular product in a busy sales period.

13 To avoid sell-outs, retailers may need to get their suppliers to s........ u........ production at short notice.

14 Zara, like Benetton and Gap, uses q........-r........ l........ to get merchandise to stores rapidly.

15 By restocking stores frequently, Zara keeps i........ c........ low.

16 RFID is unlikely to replace conventional b........ c........ for years to come.

17 Jaguar Land Rover aims to m........ the capacity of its trucks by collecting from several suppliers in the same area.

18 In order to find ways to reduce their environmental footprint, progressive companies are looking at the full l........ of their supply chain, from the design stage to the end of a product's life.

19 If a product is easy to take apart for r........, that also helps the environment.

20 Responsible companies are used to c........ with government regulations.

B **Choose the best word or phrase to complete each of these sentences.**

1 To ensure that fresh fruit arrives in good condition, it is important that the .... is not too long.
   a) travel   b) transit time   c) loading   d) driving

2 Fresh fruit and vegetables have a relatively short .... once they go on sale.
   a) shelf life   b) lifetime   c) lifecycle   d) selling time

3 Because of the increased cost of transport, companies are now having to think carefully about the .... of production plants.
   a) development   b) organisation   c) management   d) siting

4 Companies normally build new manufacturing plants because they need more ....
   a) capacity   b) profit   c) products   d) deliveries

5 Cutting costs in the production process can be achieved by using a .... strategy.
   a) total-quality   b) environmentally friendly   c) rapid-logistics   d) lean-manufacturing

6   In the future, deliveries from different suppliers will be .... so that trucks carry full loads.

    a) shorter   b) quicker   c) consolidated   d) reorganised

7   If newly launched products become very popular, they can be in .... if the logistics operation is not well planned.

    a) great demand   b) short supply   c) last position   d) great difficulty

8   To avoid shortages at peak selling times, some companies use a .... strategy rather than relying on just one supplier.

    a) just-in-time   b) bulk-shipment   c) consolidated-delivery   d) multiple-sourcing

9   Zara's production system enables it to .... quickly to changes in customer demand.

    a) respond   b) perform   c) answer   d) produce

10 To ensure its internal production operations are cost effective, Zara outsources all .... activities, such as finishing of garments, to small, local contractors.

    a) low-cost   b) cost-effective   c) labour-intensive   d) low-priority

11 RFID technology will enable retailers to know their exact .... as soon as a product is removed from the shelf.

    a) stock levels   b) cashflow   c) customer demand   d) profitability

12 Jaguar Land Rover has a 10-year goal to eliminate 90 million .... as part of its plan to reduce the impact of its supply chain on the environment.

    a) vehicles   b) containers   c) road miles   d) quality checks

13 Jaguar Land Rover and the shipping company Wallenius Wilhelmsen aim to .... fleet utilisation, so that fewer ships are needed.

    a) modernise   b) optimise   c) harmonise   d) streamline

14 With better logistics planning, it will be possible for transport companies to make better use of ...., rather than letting trucks travel empty after making a delivery.

    a) cargoes   b) drivers   c) warehouses   d) backhauls

15 Improvements in .... design mean that fewer materials are needed and more items can fit into containers, thus reducing transport costs.

    a) truck   b) packaging   c) warehouse   d) storage

16 Companies are also seeking to eliminate the use of .... and dangerous chemicals during the production process.

    a) toxic   b) unsustainable   c) expensive   d) environmental

17 It is important for their reputation that manufacturers and their suppliers have good environmental ....

    a) publicity   b) conditions   c) ideas   d) credentials

18 In some emerging countries, bribery and .... are still big problems.

    a) inefficiency   b) corruption   c) insensitivity   d) incompetence

19 Companies need to make sure that their suppliers dispose of chemicals properly, rather than just .... them somewhere.

    a) dumping   b) posting   c) removing   d) losing

20 Large companies regularly .... their suppliers, not only for quality but also to check compliance with health and safety regulations.

    a) contact   b) visit   c) assist   d) audit

Answer key

Reading

A
1 Manufacturers of consumer goods, and retailers in fashion, hi-tech and grocery sectors
2 Because it is the only way to make efficient use of global sourcing strategies, especially from China and south-east Asia.
3 Shops can be left without goods, or have the wrong goods; manufacturing companies may need to stop production because they lack essential components.
4 The aerospace and defence industries
5 When they move away from vertically integrated production and start to rely more on suppliers to deliver components for the production process
6 Because the cost of each aircraft is very high, any interruption in supply will cost a lot of money. Aerospace manufacturers also rely heavily on suppliers and partners.

B
1 Because it can increase a company's market value by between 7 and 26 per cent above the industry average.
2 Because they already have very efficient supply chains.
3 Shops can have a warehouse full of summer dresses in October; mobile phone shops can have last season's phones at the peak Christmas period.
4 More than 700 suppliers and also the suppliers of those suppliers
5 They need to know what is happening in their supply chain and have fast access to data.
6 Storms affecting shipping or a production shortfall
7 Because they are 10 years behind other industries, such as hi-tech and automotive.
8 $100m
9 Because the cost of each aircraft is so high, any problem in the supply chain that might hold up production would be very expensive.

Vocabulary

A 1 retailers   2 stock   3 store   4 warehouse   5 to source   6 shortfall   7 divert   8 vendor   9 stock-outs   10 penalties   11 tier-one suppliers   12 tier-three, -four, -five suppliers
B 1 a) efficient   b) effective
2 1 efficient   2 effective   3 effective   4 efficient
C 1 d/f   2 c   3 a   4 e   5 f/d   6 b
D 1 for   2 for   3 up   4 for   5 in   6 to   7 into   8 away from   9 against   10 for
E 1 c   2 f   3 j   4 h   5 d   6 a   7 i   8 e   9 g   10 b

Reading

A Statement 3
B
1 Head of Global Product Supply; in 2001
2 It's the world's largest supply chain.
3 They are facing big increases in raw material and energy costs.
4 To reduce costs in the supply chain
5 To produce sales growth
6 It is normally reactive and passive, focusing mainly on cost control.
7 By preventing the retailer being out of stock of products and by reducing the amount of stock carried
8 It wants something tangible in return – better pricing in the stores, better positioning and display of its goods.
9 Very important: Wal-Mart's worldwide stores account for 15 per cent of P&G's global sales.
10 Wal-Mart gives P&G access to its customer sales data. This enables P&G to deliver goods specially tailored for each store.
11 No, other suppliers also have access to the customer sales data collected by Wal-Mart's Retail Link system.
12 It is running a pilot project using Wal-Mart's live customer sales data to prepare deliveries for individual stores.

Vocabulary

A 1 a competitive edge   2 battle   3 at a premium   4 at the forefront   5 surging   6 display
7 a pilot project   8 live sales data   9 replenishment   10 assembled
B 1 inventory   2 working capital   3 replenishment deliveries   4 sales data   5 vendors   6 road congestion
7 freight costs   8 cost control   9 growth targets
C 1 to ship   2 to distribute   3 to grow   4 to improve   5 to deliver   6 to invest   7 to replenish   8 to store
9 to compete   10 to manufacture
D 1 b   2 a   3 a   4 b   5 b   6 a
E 1 is [...] divided   2 are [...] prepared   3 are moved   4 is assembled

UNIT 3

Reading

A 1 They are seen as very high-tech, high-performance products with a strong brand image, especially for
young people.
2 Almost 100 per cent
3 Highly important
4 With information systems and a logistics infrastructure to co-ordinate supply of components and
delivery of finished goods
B 1 F (*It transformed the cheapest of mass-market footwear into high-tech, high-performance products ...*
(lines 2–4))
2 T (*... the management of the supply chain is a crucial strategic issue at Nike.* (lines 10–11))
3 N (There is no reference to how many employees Nike has.)
4 F (It outsources almost 100 per cent of its production abroad, but does a lot of its design and
development in the US.)
5 T (*Nike's basketball shoe, for example, is designed in Oregon and Tennessee ...* (lines 20–21))
6 F (*The shoes themselves are manufactured in South Korea [...] and in Indonesia ...* (lines 22–24))
7 N (The basketball shoe passes through 120 pairs of hands during the production process, but we are not
told if these are checks. And we are told nothing about other products.)
8 T (*... allowing the company to bring more than 300 new shoe designs to market each year.* (lines 37–39))
9 N (This is a danger, but the article does not say whether this happens or not.)
10 T (*In the United States and Europe, primary distribution of Nike products is increasingly outsourced to
specialist third parties ...* (lines 42–44))
11 N (It has widened its portfolio to include these products, but there is no mention that it plans to move
away from its core product area of sports shoes.)

Vocabulary

A 1 a   2 b   3 a   4 b   5 b   6 b   7 a   8 b
B 1 i   2 e   3 h   4 g   5 b   6 d   7 c   8 f   9 j   10 a
C 1 lead times   2 information systems   3 business processes   4 production process   5 sales forecasts
6 order fulfilment   7 logistics infrastructure   8 manufacturing strategy   9 customer service
10 product availability
D 1 US-based   2 mass-market   3 high-performance   4 brand-led   5 globe-spanning   6 state-of-the-art
7 low-cost   8 in-house   9 far-flung   10 fashion-conscious

UNIT 4

Reading

A 1 They changed from IBM to Intel as their supplier of microprocessors, which was a huge and risky decision.
2 Cost, quality and being on time (timeliness)
3 The increasing use of just-in-time management and faster response times demanded by customers
4 A commitment (strong belief and effort) to quality
5 Sourcing in-house (internally) or through its own subsidiaries, or using external supply companies
6 They should build strong partnerships with their suppliers.
B 1 This can cause other delays in the production process, and delays have the potential to reduce profits.
2 It can expect to be more profitable (twice as profitable) and expect to grow more quickly (three times
more quickly).
3 Their own products will be late getting onto the market and have faults (defects). As a consequence of
delays and product defects, companies can also lose any price advantage they had.

4 Commitment from both the customers and the suppliers
Suppliers and customers being open with each other
Trust between customers and their suppliers

Vocabulary

A 1 g 2 h 3 e 4 f 5 c 6 j 7 b 8 i 9 a 10 d
B 1 1 entire 2 relate to 3 critical 4 widespread 5 respond 6 source 7 wholly owned
8 open 9 function
2 timeliness, knock-on delays
3 timely, on time, late to market
4 *Suggested answers*
(three weeks) late; delayed by (two weeks); (a week) behind schedule; a (two-month) delay
C 1 on time 2 knock-on delays 3 late to market 4 timeliness 5 timely
D 1 g 2 c 3 e 4 f 5 b 6 h 7 d 8 a
E 1 cause 2 respond 3 source 4 Building 5 had
F 1 **twice as** profitable **as, three times more** quickly

UNIT 5

Reading

A 1 1 T
2 F (It was in serious danger of going out of business, but its customers, including BMW, have given it support to help it survive.)
3 F (It affects a wide range of industries, from manufacturing to retail.)
2 a 4 b 3 c 5 d 2 e 1
B 1 Because it would take too long to find an alternative supplier.
2 It increased the number of staff in its risk-monitoring department who were looking only at suppliers.
3 It has set up a rating system and is in regular contact with its German competitors to share information on suppliers.
4 Production at a German car manufacturer almost stopped as result of the failure of one of its sub-suppliers (second-tier suppliers) which provided the material for its car seats.

Vocabulary

A 1 1 insolvency 2 a crisis 3 disruption 4 risk-monitoring department 5 failures 6 monitor
7 a rating system 8 an early warning system 9 interdependencies 10 goes bankrupt
2 *Suggested answers*
a) **Risk management**: risk-monitoring department, monitor, a rating system, an early warning system
b) **Company failure**: insolvency, failures, goes bankrupt
B 1 failure(s) 2 insolvency 3 insolvent 4 file for 5 become 6 bankrupt 7 go
C 1 1 d 2 e 3 a 4 b 5 c
2 Using a single supplier to supply the same component, product or service
D 1 supplier base 2 primary; second-tier 3 dual sourcing 4 Multiple sourcing 5 single sourcing
E 1 getting into difficulties/trouble 2 Set up 3 Monitor 4 maintain 5 communicate with 6 swap
7 Extend 8 switch 9 fail / go bankrupt

UNIT 6

Reading

A 1 Philips Electronics' 2 silicon chips 3 three days later 4 Nokia 5 several months 6 Nokia
7 Ericsson 8 Nokia
B 1 Its computer systems detected possible delays in shipments of chips coming from Philips.
2 It put the five components from Philips on a special monitoring list and increased monitoring of shipments from weekly to daily.
3 Executives from Nokia worked together with executives from Philips to develop alternative plans for maintaining supplies of chips for Nokia.
They also sent a team to its other chip manufacturers in the US and Japan to negotiate priority status for supplies of chips and to get them to increase production.

4 a) Short-term: lost $400m in sales
Long term: forced to stop manufacturing mobile phones
b) Short-term: managed to maintain production levels for phones all the way through the crisis
Long-term: strengthened its position as European market leader for mobile phones

Vocabulary

A 1 f   2 i   3 a   4 c   5 h   6 d   7 e   8 j   9 b   10 g
B 1 1 booming   2 accounted for   3 to secure   4 to ramp up   5 minor   6 simplifying   7 estimated
8 strengthen
2 As a matter of routine
3 *status* in line 26 = b
status in line 38 = a
C 1 b   2 c   3 a   4 f   5 d   6 e
D 1 1 of; to   2 in/at; for   3 from   4 to   5 for   6 of   7 for; of   8 of; in   9 to
2 1 c   2 a   3 b
3 Two of them [suppliers] responded *within five days* ... (lines 39–40)
Ericsson remained unaware of the potential disruption to their orders *until three days after the fire* ...
(lines 42–43)
[Philips] did not take action *until early April.* (line 45)
By then [early April], Nokia had already secured supplies. (lines 45–46)

UNIT 7

Reading

A 1 F (It was the reduction in transport costs that made it possible for manufacturers to take advantage of low
labour costs. (lines 1–6))
2 F (Research suggests that no companies have made the savings they predicted. (lines 10–13))
3 T
4 T
5 F (Only some have done this. (lines 73–75))
B 1 Proctor & Gamble reported that costs for storage and transport were higher than the operating costs in
their factories abroad.
Other companies reported that product costs in their foreign factories were lower, but that the quality was
often lower, too.
2 a) Car manufacturers setting up in Slovakia in Eastern Europe will find a shortage of trained workers and
high wage inflation as companies compete for staff.
b) In India, competition for trained staff means staff change jobs frequently to get higher salaries, and
20 per cent staff turnover is normal.
c) In China, trained middle mangers in the car industry with fluent English and Mandarin can earn more
then their counterparts in Germany and the UK.
3 a) Offshoring will decline. Increasingly, companies will bring back their manufacturing to be nearer to their
main markets.
b) Companies will have a larger number of small plants, located near to their markets and capable of
producing customised products for the specific markets.
C 1 companies that have decided to source abroad
2 the 'static' cost of a supply chain
3 the lower cost of the product
4 the product
5 companies not considering or underestimating other costs
6 the belief that there is an unlimited supply of labour in Eastern Europe, India and China
7 workers in China and India
8 in emerging countries

Vocabulary

A 1 d 2 h 3 g 4 j 5 b 6 i 7 f 8 e 9 c 10 a

B 1 1 e 2 c 3 a 4 f 5 b 6 d
2 transport cost, product cost, labour cost, unit cost
3 *Suggested answers*
inventory cost, distribution cost, shipping cost, raw material cost, manufacturing cost

C 1 a) global sourcing b) operating expenses c) wage inflation
2 a) emerging countries b) low-cost labour c) trained workers
3 a) customised products b) local market
4 buffer stocks
5 cost efficiencies

D 1 estimated 2 tend 3 offsets 4 ignore 5 underestimate 6 assume 7 remain stable 8 exhausted

E 1 b 2 d

F 1 1 offshoring 2 offshore 3 operation(s) 4 operating 5 sourcing 6 source 7 sourcing
8 manufacturing 9 manufacture 10 manufactured

UNIT 8

Reading tasks

A 1 Statement c
2 It will keep its position.
3 e, c, a

B 1 It has a growing market of more than 1 billion people. It has become the third largest manufacturer in the world.
2 Labour costs in Singapore are two-and-a-half times higher.
3 Because labour costs represent only a small proportion of the total cost of computer assembly, and production costs were lower in Singapore.
4 Because government officials at provincial level have a lot of power and compete with each other and central government, making it hard for foreign manufacturers to negotiate a single agreement for the whole country.
5 China is too far away. Forty per cent of its production is customised, which means it needs to have its production located nearby so that it can respond quickly to customer requirements.

C Explanation b

Vocabulary

A 1 f 2 g 3 a 4 b 5 h 6 c 7 d 8 i 9 e

B 1 1 d 2 a 3 c 4 b
2 1 investment, expert, centre 2 costs, charges 3 officials 4 plants

C 1 labour costs 2 industrialised countries 3 operating plants 4 technical sophistication
5 manufacturing investment 6 competitive edge 7 global manufacturing 8 freight charges/costs

D 1 1 status 2 to set up 3 appeal 4 concern 5 pitfalls 6 single 7 shifts 8 splitting
9 makes most sense
2 expanding
3 *Suggested answers*
contracting, shrinking, decreasing

E 1 shifts 2 pitfalls 3 appeal; concern 4 make sense 5 set up 6 split

UNIT 9

Reading

A 1 a) They had subcontracted work to home workers who used child labour.
b) It was paying very low wages.
2 It cancelled the contracts with the suppliers.
3 The supply-chain expert and the executive
4 The executive

B 1 S 2 S (also implied by A) 3 S, E 4 A 5 S 6 E 7 A

Vocabulary

A 1 deception   2 violations   3 allegations   4 neglect   5 a living wage   6 guarantee   7 margins
8 audits   9 corporate social responsibility practices   10 spot checks   11 codes of conduct   12 on-site

B 1 f   2 c   3 d   4 a   5 b   6 e

C 1 audit   2 carries out   3 exposes   4 cancelling   5 a) fire   b) adhere to   c) used/employed

D 1 a) allegations   b) employment practices
2 auditors
3 audits
4 ethical
5 a) code   b) working conditions   c) living wage   d) child labour
6 a) inspections   b) subcontractors

E 1 a) in   b) in   2 on   3 a) down   b) to   c) of   4 with   5 with   6 a) in   b) in

---

UNIT 10

Reading

A 1 Having 'exotic' fruit and vegetables from the tropics available in shops in the UK and other northern countries
2 The supply chain for fresh produce that needs to be kept at a cool temperature
3 It is more time sensitive; in other words, it needs to be transported quickly to the supermarket shelves.
4 Being careful to keep temperature fluctuations to a minimum, having good ventilation and transporting the products as quickly as possible
5 In less than 48 hours

B 1 Reefer containers. *Reefer* is used as a kind of short form of *refrigeration*.
2 It can control everything from temperature and humidity to ventilation and gas levels.
3 They detect temperature or other problems and fix them during the voyage, sending alerts to the vessel's bridge or to a website through which shippers can make adjustments remotely.
4 An order is placed in the evening to suppliers. The fruit and vegetables are picked and packed the next day. They are sent that evening to the distribution centre. The following morning they can be on the supermarket shelves.
5 High-value produce, such as soft fruit
6 At Heathrow Airport
7 Christian Salvesen
8 More than 90,000 tonnes
9 Fresh produce is sorted by type or destination and price/product labels are printed.
10 There would have been three to four handling points in the supply chain instead of just one now.

Vocabulary

A 1 monitored   2 detect   3 alerts   4 adjustments   5 fluctuations   6 transit time   7 perishable
8 produce   9 shelf life   10 condensed   11 chilled   12 bulk shipments   13 sell-by date

B 1 relies on   2 cut [...] out of   3 moved on   4 looking beyond   5 speeded up   6 broken up

C 1 1 i   2 g   3 e   4 a   5 h   6 c   7 b/d   8 j   9 d/b   10 f
2 1 f   2 e   3 a   4 c   5 g   6 d   7 b

D 1 control the temperature   2 satisfy [...] demand   3 problems [...] detected; make adjustments
4 order [...] placed   5 print labels; change prices

UNIT 11

Reading

A 1 It has been based on large, regional production sites with big transportation distances to the customer.
2 It is carrying out a full review of its supply operations, asking the question: 'What is our business going to look like in 2015?'
3 Trends such as smaller product sizes, sustainable packaging, future consumer demand by region, as well as factors such as the price of oil and road-congestion issues

B 1 It is considering moving its production sites closer to consumers.
2 In the 1980s and 1990s
3 $10 a barrel

4 He says that P&G's supply-chain design 'is now upside down' because of much higher oil prices.
5 To review in detail the design of its supply operations
6 Reductions in product size, sustainable packaging and future consumer demand based on regions, as well as changes in the global operating environment
7 What happens if oil is $200 a barrel? What happens if you can't ship using trucks on the weekends or if there are road-congestion issues? Or if you can't bring trucks into cities any more?
8 Manufacturing sites producing only one type of product for a very big geographical region, which means that transport distances are very long
9 When oil went beyond $70 a barrel
10 It is having to think carefully about where it locates its production plants in future.
11 It has global sales of $80bn. It operates 145 manufacturing plants worldwide and has about 30,000 trucks on the road every day
12 The cost of transportation to distribute goods to the customer set against the location of a manufacturing plant

C a) the price of a barrel of oil in the 1980s and 1990s
b) the date for P&G's study to forecast what their business will look like
c) a possible future price of a barrel of oil
d) P&G's global sales
e) the price of a barrel of oil below which P&G could not justify building new capacity
f) the maximum price of a barrel of oil at the time this article was written
g) the number of trucks P&G has on the road around the world every day
h) the number of manufacturing plants operated by P&G

Vocabulary

A 1 soaring   2 to rethink   3 shifting   4 to cut   5 era   6 implemented   7 capital spending   8 capacity   9 upside down   10 review   11 kicked off   12 to anticipate   13 road congestion   14 to justify   15 siting

B 1 shifting; soaring   2 era   3 rethink   4 kicked off; anticipate   5 road congestion   6 justify   7 siting   8 implemented   9 review   10 cut   11 upside down   12 capital spending   13 capacity

C 1 a; c   2 e; g   3 b; f   4 k   5 c   6 i   7 h   8 j   9 l   10 f   11 a   12 d

D 1 1 distribute   2 manufacture   3 produce   4 consume   5 transport   6 spend   7 expand   8 calculate
2 1 implementation   2 development/developer   3 assessment/assessor   4 reduction   5 justification   6 shipment/ship/shipper   7 operation/operator   8 location

E manufacturing sites, production sites, manufacturing plants, factories, facility

UNIT 12

Reading

A 1 Just-in-time, lean manufacturing and low-cost country sourcing
2 Inventory will be stored closer to the customer. Products will be shipped to shared warehouses close to consumers, and shared transport will deliver to city hubs for final distribution to stores.
3 The concern to reduce CO_2 emissions, reduce energy consumption for transport and reduce traffic congestion

B 1 T (It was at a time when oil prices were much lower than today, and climate change was not a topic for discussion.)
2 N (Nothing is mentioned about this.)
3 F (They are part of the traditional supply chain strategy and must be re-evaluated.)
4 F (Tipping-point analysis assesses when it is right to store goods closer to the customer and when just-in-time delivery is still the best choice.)
5 T (Because they are low-cost, bulky products, it is not economic to store them close to the customer.)
6 N (It is certainly moving in that direction, but nothing is mentioned about whether it is a leader in this.)
7 T (Having one larger warehouse rather than several smaller ones is much more energy efficient as far as the storage of goods is concerned.)
8 F (Generally, cost reduction and carbon reduction go together.)
9 T (This is the recommendation of the report *The 2016 Future Supply Chain*.)
10 N (The current supply-chain designs are aimed at improving on-shelf availability. It doesn't say whether this will apply to the new model.)

Vocabulary

A 1 tied up 2 in the light of 3 end-to-end 4 tipping point 5 bulky 6 trade-off
7 vehicle loading 8 empty running 9 off-peak periods 10 carbon footprint 11 merged
12 parameters 13 consolidated

B 1 bulky 2 carbon footprint 3 off-peak 4 empty running 5 vehicle loading 6 tied up
7 parameters 8 trade-off 9 consolidated 10 merged 11 tipping point 12 in the light of
13 end-to-end

C 1 on 2 in 3 at; of 4 in; of 5 at 6 on 7 to 8 between 9 from; to 10 to 11 by 12 to

D 1 c ii 2 a iii 3 b i

UNIT 13

Reading

A 1 new products that become very popular 2 underestimate demand 3 sees
4 making their supply chains more flexible
2 a) 4 b) 2 c) 1 d) 3

B 1 Customers will get a bad impression of the company and be unwilling to buy from it again.
Companies will lose potential sales.
Companies will be left with unwanted stock if demand for the product has decreased by the time
the stock is replaced.
2 It has one plant in Vancouver, near to the US market, to meet temporary increases in demand, and
another in lower-cost Singapore for high-volume production.
3 a) one week b) four weeks
4 Toyota shows continuous production reports in its plants.
Dell updates managers hourly on production.

Vocabulary

A 1 1 d 2 f 3 e 4 j 5 h 6 b 7 a 8 i 9 c 10 g
2 sell-outs, ration, withhold, run out of, scarce
3 noun: sell-outs (of products/goods)
verbs: withhold, ration, run out of (stock)
adjective: scarce (products/goods)
4 *Scarce* means the same as 'in short supply'.

B 1 scarce 2 ration; withhold 3 running out 4 sell-outs 5 in short supply

C 1 1 a) decrease b) rapidly 2 a) boost/step up b) surges 3 a) Broadening
b) step up/boost c) quickly/rapidly
2 *Suggested answers*
1 rise, upsurge, growth, upturn, reduction, fall, drop, plunge
2 raise, expand, lower, reduce, cut, slow down
3 slowly, gradually, steadily

D 1 1 right 2 tough/ hard 3 sophisticated 4 actual 5 closer 6 costly
7 accurate 8 common 9 responsive 10 free
2 predictions (lines 74–75)

E 1 a) to b) at 2 a) in b) in c) up to 3 of 4 a) by b) with 5 from 6 on

---

UNIT 14

Reading

A 1 T
2 T
3 F (It imports 20 per cent of its merchandise from Asia Pacific as finished goods. (lines 16–19))
4 F (Some manufacturing is done in Zara's own factories, such as cutting and dyeing, but the rest of
the manufacturing is done by a network of small, local sub-contractors. (lines 28–32))
5 T
6 F (It uses specialist shipping contractors. (lines 43–45))
7 F (It prefers them to have too little rather than too much stock. (lines 49–50))
8 T

B 1 1 18–35-year-old women 2 Gap, Mango (another Spanish fashion retailer) and Benetton
3 to minimise stock levels and to respond quickly to market needs 4 La Coruña and Zaragoza

2 1 cutting
   2 small subcontractors located near to Zara's headquarters in north-west Spain
   3 price-tagging
   4 Zara's two distribution centres in La Coruña and Zaragoza
   5 Zara's headquarters in La Coruña
   6 specialist shipping contractors

Vocabulary

A 1 1 e   2 i   3 a   4 h   5 g   6 d   7 f   8 c   9 b
B 1 1 needs   2 countries/systems/activities   3 process   4 costs   5 centres   6 cycle
   2 stock allocations, price tag, air freight
C 1 production process   2 stock allocations   3 price tags   4 inventory costs   5 distribution centres
   6 delivery cycle
D 1 c   2 g   3 d   4 a   5 f   6 e   7 b
E 1 1 is imported   2 are done by
   2 Finished goods **are sent** to … (line 40)
      … they **are labelled, price-tagged** […] and **packed.** (lines 41–43)
      … they **are carried** by specialist contractors … (lines 43–44)
      Road **is used** for journeys … air freight **is used** for longer distances. (lines 45–46)
      All deliveries **are completed** … (lines 46–47)
      Stock allocations […] **are calculated** centrally … (line 48)
      … production **is** always **kept** at a level … (lines 49–50)
   3 1 are given   2 is sourced   3 is cut; dyed   4 are attached
F 1 b   2 c   3 d   4 a

UNIT 15

Before you read

1 a) 3   b) 2   c) 1

Reading

A 1 1 already   2 partially   3 pallets and cases of products   4 reduce operating costs   5 for many years
   6 invests a lot
B 1 a) When Metro first started to use RFID technology
      b) The number of Metro's distribution centres using RFID technology (at the time of writing)
      c) The number of Metro's suppliers using RFID at pallet level
         The approximate number of new applications Metro is working on at its Innovation Centre
      d) The total number of Metro's locations
      e) The unit price for RFID chips that would make the technology a realistic option for companies
      f) The year when Metro started testing RFID applications
      g) The number of technology partners Metro is working with
   2 1 a) Metro tests new RFID applications in a real supermarket situation.
         b) Neuss is the location of its RFID Innovation Centre. At the centre, it develops new applications
            for its business operations and consumers, and collaborates with partners like IBM and Intel to
            develop the technology.
      2 a) The 'smart shelf' will help supermarket staff know when to restock shelves.
         b) The 'smart fridge' will help consumers know when products have passed their expiry date and are
            no longer safe to eat.

Vocabulary

A 1 1 b   2 e   3 f   4 a   5 g   6 d   7 c
B 1 tags/technology/applications   2 losses   3 centre   4 experience   5 operations   6 partners
C 1 a) RFID technology   b) logistics operations
   2 a) RFID tags   b) inventory losses
   3 a) innovation centre   b) RFID applications   c) retail operations   d) shopping experience
D 1 refill   2 fall   3 experiment   4 follow   5 act with   6 grow   7 join   8 make
E 1 state-of-the-art   2 conventional   3 ultimate   4 individual   5 certain   6 viable
   7 huge   8 innovative
F 1 a) in   b) since   2 a) to   b) on   3 a) of   b) to   4 a) with   b) for   5 a) out   b) at   c) in

UNIT 16

Reading

A 1 In 2003, JLR did not know the carbon footprint of its supply chain. Since then, it has set itself targets to reduce carbon emissions by optimising its transport system, using rail instead of road where possible and using efficient ship transportation.

2 It is a system of collecting components from five or six suppliers in the same geographical area in order to maximise the capacity of the trailer and so reduce road miles.

3 By running vessels at lower speeds and by using low-sulphur fuel.

B 1 In 2003   2 186,076 tonnes a year   3 To eliminate 90m road miles   4 Tata Motors

5 290,000   6 To reduce costs

7 It has reduced CO_2 emissions by 1,772 tonnes a year.

8 By using next-generation truck engines

9 The purchase price is just the cost of the materials without taking account of transport. The total landed cost takes into account freight, packaging, customs and other costs associated with transport.

10 By switching from road to rail for transporting finished vehicles

11 By paying extra for ships to use low-sulphur fuel

12 A project to build a lightweight, environmentally friendly cargo ship that will be powered by a combination of solar, wind and wave power, and therefore will not release any emissions into the atmosphere or the ocean.

Vocabulary

A 1 are on target   2 set up   3 specified   4 implications   5 streamlined   6 reviewing
7 lightweight   8 environmentally sound

B 1 set up   2 implications   3 reviewing   4 lightweight   5 is on target
6 environmentally sound   7 specified   8 streamline

C 1 by   2 a) per   b) from   c) to   3 by   4 to   5 a) Between   b) by   6 per

D 1 f   2 d   3 a   4 g   5 b   6 c   7 e

E 1 logistics contract   2 road miles   3 fleet utilisation   4 carbon footprint   5 supplier base
6 purchase price   7 vehicle delivery

F 1 streamline, optimise, maximise, improve
2 cut, reduce, eliminate

UNIT 17

Reading

A Statement c

B 1 Transportation of goods

2 At every stage, even back to the design stage

3 25 to 30 per cent of vehicles travel empty due to poor scheduling of deliveries.

4 Transportation by ship

5 By looking again at where products are made and stored, and where suppliers are located

6 Because they may have to combine two sets of warehouses and transport systems, leading to overlap and duplication.

7 They are looking at the full lifecycle of their entire supply chain, assessing the use of energy and materials at each stage, from design through to recycling at the end of a product's life.

8 By reducing or eliminating the use of toxic chemicals during production, and by making the product easier to take apart at the recycling stage

9 By cutting down on materials used, and by making transportation of products more environmentally friendly because more items can be fitted into a container

Vocabulary

A 1 b   2 a   3 b   4 b   5 a   6 b   7 a   8 a

B 1 c/d/k   2 a/f   3 h   4 j   5 i   6 c/d/k   7 b   8 a/f   9 e   10 g   11 c/d/k

C 1 focus on   2 iron out   3 run around   4 end up   5 work out   6 pointed out   7 put back
8 look for   9 go back   10 take apart   11 cut down on

D 1 inappropriate   2 unsustainable   3 irrelevant   4 invisible   5 unnecessary
6 unprogressive

UNIT 18

Reading

A 1 Consumers
2 Suppliers, too, need to be environmentally sensitive; companies need to check that their suppliers are operating in an environmentally sensitive way.
3 Because the number of factories and immigrant workers is too large for local inspectors to deal with.
4 They are likely to become more successful in the market.

B 1 F (*... there's been a shift from the government driving this, to the customer.* (lines 13–15))
2 T ('*Consumers are looking to businesses to improve their environmental credentials.*' (lines 15–17))
3 F (*... companies are used to dealing with compliance regulations* [...] *But they now face the problem of meeting the ethical expectations of customers as well.* (lines 1–7))
4 N (Greenpeace accused them of this, but we don't know for sure.)
5 T (*... and that means choosing suppliers that can also prove the environmental credentials of their suppliers.* (lines 29–32))
6 N (HP is clearly putting a lot of effort into this, but nothing is stated about whether it is the leader in this area.)
7 T (*On her way to China to test how green 60 of the company's suppliers really are ...* (lines 38–40))
8 F (*Maybe there is corruption or bribery.* (lines 51–52))
9 T (*The infrastructure isn't there to deal with that many factories, so we have our own health and safety officers.* (lines 55–58))
10 F (*... Dell, Intel, Apple, HP, Sun and others have signed up to the Electronic Industry Code of Conduct, an initiative to improve conditions in the electronics supply chain ...* (lines 72–76))

Vocabulary

A 1 f   2 d   3 j   4 i   5 g   6 a   7 c   8 h   9 e   10 b
B 1 to   2 at/to   3 towards   4 of   5 out   6 with   7 up   8 up to
C 1 picks up   2 look to   3 signed up to   4 are used to   5 find out   6 deal with
7 is turning towards   8 be aware of   9 look [carefully] at
D 1 1 sourcing/source   2 publisher/publication/publishing   3 improvement
4 criticism/critic   5 choice   6 exploitation   7 auditor/audit   8 inspector/inspection
9 achievement   10 proof
2 1 comply with   2 consume   3 corrupt   4 bribe   5 dispose of   6 expect   7 regulate   8 initiate
E 1 comply with   2 auditor   3 improvement   4 are disposed of   5 consumes   6 proof   7 expect

CHECK TEST 1

A 1 Components   2 warehouses   3 cost-control   4 inventory   5 working capital   6 bottom-line
7 supply-chain management   8 stock-outs   9 competitive edge   10 demand   11 First-tier
12 supply base   13 Single sourcing   14 buffer stocks   15 just-in-time   16 relationships
17 lead time   18 outsourcing   19 in-house   20 code of conduct
B 1 a   2 d   3 b   4 a   5 b   6 d   7 a   8 d   9 b   10 a   11 c   12 b   13 c   14 d   15 c   16 b
17 a   18 d   19 a   20 b

CHECK TEST 2

A 1 Perishable   2 containers   3 air-freighted   4 sell-by-date   5 transporting   6 production sites
7 carbon footprint   8 emissions   9 Road congestion   10 Empty running   11 off-peak
12 run out   13 step up   14 quick-response logistics   15 inventory costs   16 bar codes
17 maximise   18 lifecycle   19 recycling   20 complying
B 1 b   2 a   3 d   4 a   5 d   6 c   7 b   8 d   9 a   10 c   11 a   12 c   13 b   14 d   15 b   16 a
17 d   18 b   19 a   20 d

Glossary

A

access *n.* the opportunity to have or use something that will bring you benefits

accessible *adj.* easy for anyone to obtain or use

account for *v.* to form a particular amount or part of something

adhere *v.* to obey a rule, law of agreement

adjustment *n.* a change that is made to something in order to correct or improve it

air-freight *n.* the system of carrying goods by plane

air-freighted *adj.* carried by air

alert *n.* a warning to be ready for possible danger

alienate *v.* to do something that makes someone unwilling to support you

allegation *n.* a statement that someone has done something wrong or illegal, but that has not been proved

anticipate *v.* to expect that something will happen and be ready for it

appeal *n.* a quality that makes people like or want to buy something

application *n.* a practical use for something

assemble *v.* to fit together all the separate parts of something

assess *v.* to make a judgement about situation after considering all the information

audit *n.* an official examination of the quality or standard of a particular part of an organisation's activities or performance

audit *v.* to officially examine the quality or standard of particular part of an organisation's activities or performance

auditor *n.* a person whose job is to officially audit an aspect of an organisation's activities, such as quality and working conditions

B

backhaul *n.* the return journey of a vehicle that transports goods after it has delivered its load

bankrupt *adj.* not having enough money to pay your debts, especially when this has been decided by a court

bankruptcy *n.* when someone is judged to be unable to pay their debts by a court of law, and their assets are shared among the people and businesses that they owe money to

bar code *n.* a series of lines printed on products sold in a shop that can be read by a machine connected to a computer to give the price, keep a record of the sale, etc.

barge *n.* a large, low boat with a flat bottom, used for carrying goods on a canal or river

boost *v.* to increase something in strength, number or value

bottom-line *adj.* the degree of profit or loss after everything has been calculated

breach *n.* an action that breaks an agreement, rule, law, etc.

break up *v.* to separate something into several smaller parts

bribery *n.* illegally giving money to someone to persuade them to do something to help you

buffer stocks *n.pl.* an extra quantity of goods that is kept in order to protect against possible interruptions to supplies

bulk shipment *n.* a delivery of a large amount of goods, such as grain or coal, usually loose, in a large ship

bulky *adj.* Something that is *bulky* is bigger than other things of its type and is difficult to carry or store.

bunker fuel *n.* the type of fuel oil used to power a ship

C

capacity *n.* **1** the amount of space a container has to hold things

2 the amount of goods that a factory can produce or deal with

carbon footprint *n.* a measurement of the amount of carbon dioxide (CO_2) that a company's activities produce

cargo haulage *n.* the business or activity of carrying goods by road or rail

cashflow *n.* the amounts of money coming into and going out of a company, and the timing of these

centralised *adj.* when a part of an organisation's activities is controlled from one particular place, e.g. its distribution or warehousing

charge *n.* an amount of money paid for services or goods

chilled *adj.* when food is kept at a low temperature so that it becomes colder but does not freeze

climate change *n.* changes that are thought to be affecting the world's weather so that it is becoming warmer

code of conduct *n.* a set of rules that employees, companies or professional people agree to follow in the way they behave and do business

collaborative *adj.* involving, or done by, several people or groups of people working together; shared between several groups

commitment *n.* the hard work and loyalty that someone gives to an organisation or activity

committed *adj.* loyal to a belief and willing to work hard for it

common *adj.* If something is *common*, it is used or shared by two or more things.

compelling *adj.* an argument, etc. that makes you feel certain that something is true or that you must do something about it

compete *v.* When one company or country *competes* with another, it tries to get people to buy its goods or services rather than those available from another company or country.

competition *n.* a situation in which businesses are trying to be more successful than others by selling more goods and services and making more profit

competitive edge *n.* a clear advantage that makes one company more successful than other companies it competes with

competitor *n.* a product, company, country, etc. that is competing with another

compliance *n.* when someone obeys a law or rule or keeps an agreement

comply (with) *v.* to obey a rule or law or to keep to an agreement

component *n.* one of several parts that together make up a whole product, machine, etc.

condensed *adj.* made shorter or smaller

configuration *n.* the shape or arrangement of the parts of something

congestion *n.* a situation when roads are so full of vehicles that the traffic cannot move properly

consistency *n.* the quality of always happening in the same way and having the same standard

consolidate *v.* to join things together into one, especially organisations, departments and business activities

consolidation *n.* when companies combine parts of their business activities in takeovers and mergers

consumer *n.* a person who buys goods, products and services for their own use, not for business use or to resell

consumer goods *n.pl.* goods bought by people for their own use, rather than by businesses and organisations

consumption *n.* the amount of goods, services, energy or natural materials used in a particular period of time

container *n.* a very large metal box, of a standard size, in which goods are packed to make it easy to lift or move them onto a ship or road vehicle

contaminate *v.* to make something dirty and dangerous, for example with chemicals or poison

continuity *n.* the state of continuing for a period of time, without problems, interruptions or changes

contract *n.* a formal written agreement between two or more people or groups which says what each must do for the other, or must not do

controversy *n.* a serious argument about something that involves many people and continues for a long time

core customers *n.pl.* the main customers of a company or organisation

corporate social responsibility (CSR) *n.* the idea that a company's role is not just about producing goods, but that it has a duty to help people in society

corruption *n.* when someone who has power or authority uses it in a dishonest or illegal way to get money or an advantage

cost control *n.* the process of making sure that a company does not spend too much

cost-efficiency *n.* the act of saving money by making a product or performing an activity in a better way

credentials *n.pl.* a company's achievements or experience that prove it has the ability to do a particular task

crisis *n.* a difficult situation that must be dealt with quickly so that the situation does not get worse

critical *adj.* Something that is *critical* is very important because what happens in the future depends on it.

customised *adj.* If something is *customised* for a customer, it is designed, built, etc. especially for that customer, making it different to other things of the same kind.

customs *n.pl.* the place at an airport or port through which people and goods arriving in a country must pass and where any tax owed must be paid

D

damage *v.* to cause physical harm to something

data *n.pl.* information in a form that can be stored and used, especially on a computer

deception *n.* the act of deliberately making someone believe something that is not true

defect *n.* a fault in something or the way it has been made that means it is not perfect

delay *n.* when something does not happen or start when it should

deliver *v.* to take goods to a place

delivery *n.* the act or process of bringing goods to a particular place or person

demand *n.* **1** the desire or need of customers for goods and services which they want to buy **2** the amount of spending on goods and services by companies and people in a particular economy

destroy *v.* to damage something so badly that it no longer exists or cannot be used or repaired

detect *v.* to notice or discover something, especially something that is not easy to see, hear, etc.

display *n.* an attractive arrangement of products for people to look at or buy in a shop

disposal *n.* when you get rid of something, especially something that is difficult to get rid of

disruption *n.* a situation in which something is prevented from continuing in its usual way

distribute *v.* to make goods available to customers after they have been produced

distribution *n.* the actions involved in making goods available to customers after they have been produced, for example moving, storing and selling the goods

distribution centre *n.* a large warehouse that receives goods from factories and suppliers, and sends them to shops/stores or customers

divert *v.* to send in a direction different from the planned or intended one

dual sourcing *n.* when a company has two suppliers for the same product so as to be sure that the product will always be available and to be able to compare the suppliers' prices, etc.

dump *v.* to get rid of something you do not want, especially in a place which is not suitable

E

early warning system *n.* a system set up to detect potential problems

economics *n.pl.* calculations of whether an activity or business will be profitable or not

economy of scale *n.* the financial advantages of producing something in very large quantities

effective *adj.* working well and producing the result or effect that was wanted or intended

efficiencies *n.pl.* the amounts of money, supplies, etc. that are saved by finding a better or cheaper way of doing something

efficiency *n.* the ability to do something well, without wasting time, money or energy

efficient *adj.* doing something well and thoroughly with no waste of time, money or energy

eliminate *v.* to get rid of something unnecessary or unwanted

emissions *n.pl.* harmful gases that are sent out into the air

employment practices *n.pl.* the accepted way that work is done in a particular company, organisation or country (also called **working practices**)

empty running *n.* when trucks run without carrying goods

environment *n.* the air, water and land on Earth

environmental *adj.* concerning or affecting the air, land or water on Earth

environmental impact *n.* the effect that something such as business activity can have on the environment

environmentally sound *adj.* Products or manufacturing processes that are *environmentally sound* are not harmful to the environment.

estimate *v.* to calculate what you think the value, size, amount, etc. of something is or will probably be

ethical *adj.* connected with beliefs and principles about what is right and wrong

exhaust *v.* If you *exhaust* a supply of something, you use it all, so that there is none left.

expand *v.* If an industry, organisation or business activity *expands*, it gets bigger or more successful.

expiry date *n.* the last date that a product, especially food, should be sold

exploit *v.* to use something fully and effectively in order to gain an advantage

expose *v.* to reveal the truth about someone or something that was hidden, especially when it involves something illegal, dishonest or wrong

ex-supplier factory *adj.* An *ex-supplier factory* price is one where the supplier makes goods available to the buyer at the supplier's factory, and the buyer is responsible for paying for the transport of the goods to where they are needed.

extend *v.* to make something affect more organisations, people or areas, etc. than before

extraction *n.* the process of removing or obtaining something from something else

F

facility *n.* an area or large building that is used to make or provide a particular product or service, e.g. storage/production facility

fail *v.* If a business *fails*, it is not successful and loses so much money that it has to close.

failure *n.* a situation in which a business that is not successful has to close because it is losing money

file (for) *v.* to officially ask a court for something, for example to officially state that you are insolvent (unable to pay your creditors)

finished goods *n.pl.* goods that have been made completely and are ready to be sold

fleet *n.* a group of vehicles, planes or ships owned by one company

fleet utilisation *n.* the effective use a company's fleet of trucks, planes or ships

fluctuations *n.pl.* frequent changes in the amount or level of something

forecast *n.* a description of what is likely to happen in the future, based on information that is available now

forecast *v.* to make a statement saying what is likely to happen in the future, based on information that is available now

freight *n.* goods carried in large quantities by ship, plane, train, etc.

fuel *n.* a substance such as coal, gas, or oil that can be burned to produce heat or energy

fuel efficient *adj.* A *fuel-efficient* engine or vehicle burns fuel in a more effective way than usual, so that it uses less fuel.

function *v.* If a machine or system *functions*, it works or operates in the way that it is supposed to.

G

garment *n.* a piece of clothing

generate *v.* to produce or cause something

global *adj.* affecting or involving the whole world

globe-spanning *adj.* existing all over the world

goods *n.pl.* things that are produced in order to be used or sold

green *adj.* connected with protecting the environment or harming it as little as possible

guarantee *v.* to promise that something will happen

guarantee *n.* a firm promise that something will happen

H

handling centre *n.* a large warehouse for collecting and organising the distribution of products, such as fruit and vegetables

handling point *n.* a place in the supply chain where goods need to be handled, e.g. when packing, loading and unloading, etc.

hazardous *adj.* dangerous, especially to people's health or safety

heavy industry *n.* industry that produces large goods such as cars and machines, or materials such as coal, steel or chemicals

high-performance *adj.* that can go very fast or do complicated things

high-tech *adj.* *High-tech* equipment or activities involve or use advanced technology.

I

implement *v.* to take action or make changes that you have officially decided should happen

in short supply *adj.* when not enough of a product is available

industrialised *adj.* An *industrialised* country or place has a lot of factories, mines, etc.

industry average *n.* the usual level for companies in a particular industry sector

infrastructure *n.* the basic systems and structures that an industry or business needs to work successfully

in-house *adj.* If a job is done *in-house*, it is done within an organisation, especially by the organisation's own staff.

initiative *n.* an important new plan for solving a particular problem or for achieving a particular aim

innovation *n.* the introduction of new ideas or methods

innovative *adj.* an innovative product, technology, application, etc. is new, different and better than those that existed before

insolvency *n.* a situation in which a person or a company is insolvent

insolvent *adj.* A person or company that is *insolvent* does not have enough money or assets to pay what they owe.

inspect *v.* to visit a organisation or factory officially to check that everything is satisfactory and all the rules are being obeyed

inspection *n.* an official visit to an organisation or factory to check that everything is satisfactory and all rules are being obeyed

interdependency *n.* a situation in which people or things depend on each other

inventory *n.* the amount of stock, including raw material, supplies and finished goods, that a company has at a particular time

investment *n.* when money is put into a business in order to make it more successful and profitable

iron out *v.* to solve or get rid of problems or difficulties, especially small ones

item *n.* a single thing, especially something that is for sale

J

joint venture *n.* a business activity in which two or more companies have invested together

just-in-time *adj.* If goods are produced, bought or delivered using a *just-in-time* system, they are produced, bought or delivered just before they are needed, reducing the cost to the firm of keeping goods for long periods of time.

K

knock-on delays *n.pl.* subsequent delays that happen as a result of an initial delay

L

label *n.* piece of paper or another material that is attached to something and gives information about it

labour-intensive *adj.* needing a lot of workers in order to produce something

labour *n.* all the people who work for a company or in a country

lead time *n.* the time between receiving an order and delivering the product to the customer

leading-edge *adj.* *Leading-edge* products or systems, etc. are the most modern and advanced ones available.

lean manufacturing *n.* a method of production that aims to cut costs while keeping quality high by producing only the quantity of goods that has been ordered and by reducing the amount of time and space that the production process uses

level *n.* the measured amount of something that exists at a particular time

lifecycle *n.* the period of time that something, especially a product, system or procedure, lasts or remains useful

living wage *n.* money you earn for work that is enough to pay for the basic things that you need to live

local *adj.* connected with a particular area, especially the area where something is produced

locate *v.* to be based in a particular place

logistics *n.pl.* the arrangements that are needed for goods, materials, equipment and people to be in the right place at the right time

lower *v.* to reduce something in amount, level, etc.

low-sulphur fuel *n.* fuel that contains low levels of sulphur, which is less harmful to the environment

M

manufacture *v.* to make goods in large quantities in a factory

manufacturer *n.* a company that makes products in a factory

manufacturing *n.* the business of making goods in large quantities, especially in factories

margin *n.* the difference between the price that something is sold for and the cost of producing or buying it

market *n.* a particular country, area or group of people to which a company sells or hopes to sell its goods or services

market *v.* to sell something by considering what customers need or want when buying a product or service

market value *n.* the value of the shares of a particular company

marketplace *n.* the part of the economy that involves buying and selling

mass-market *adj.* designed for sale to as wide a range of people as possible

materials *n.pl.* things you need to make or do something

maximise *v.* to increase something as much as possible; to make the best use of something

measures *n.pl.* official action, taken to deal with a particular problem

merchandise *n.* goods that are produced in order to be sold, especially goods that are sold in a store

merge *v.* when two or more companies or organisations combine to form one bigger organisation

minimise *v.* to reduce something to the lowest amount possible

monitor *v.* to carefully watch and check a situation in order to see how it changes or progresses over a period of time

multiple-sourcing *n.* getting materials or goods from a number of different suppliers (also known as **multi-sourcing**)

must-have products *n.pl.* products that are so good, interesting, fashionable, etc. that people want to own them

N

notice *n.* information or a warning given in advance of something that is going to happen

O

off-peak *adj.* Off-peak hours or periods are the times when fewer people want to do or use something.

official *n.* someone who has a responsible position in an organisation

offset *v.* to balance the effect of something, with the result that there is no real change or difference

offshore *v.* If a company *offshores* jobs or an activity, it moves them to a foreign country where costs are lower.

on-shelf availability *n.* having products on display and available for sale in a shop

operate *v.* If a business, system, etc. *operates* in or from a particular place, it is based there or offers goods or services from there.

operation *n.* a part of a business or company that does a particular activity or type of work

operational *adj.* related to the running of a business or part of a business

operations *n.pl.* a company's normal activities related to providing services or producing goods

optimise *v.* to make the best possible use of something or to do something in the best possible way

order fulfilment *n.* the act of supplying the full amount of something that a customer has asked for

order *n.* a request by a customer for goods or services

outsource *v.* If a company or organisation *outsources* its work, it employs another company to do it.

ownership structure *n.* the way in which a company is owned and controlled

P

packaging *n.* material or boxes used for wrapping goods to protect them, for example because they are being taken somewhere

pallet *n.* a flat, wooden frame used for storing and moving goods

parameters *n.pl.* a set of fixed limits that control the way something is done

partnership *n.* a relationship between two people or organisations that work together

payment terms *n.pl.* the conditions of a sales agreement that concern how the customer will pay, and especially how much time is allowed for payment

PDA (personal digital assistant) *n.* a very small, light computer that you can carry with you

penalty *n.* an amount of money someone has to pay if they do not keep to a legal agreement, for example being late in delivery of a product

perishable *adj.* likely to become bad if not kept in the proper conditions (usually referring to food products)

pick up *v.* to collect something or someone from somewhere

pilot project *n.* a project done on a small scale to find out if it will be successful

pitfall *n.* a problem or difficulty that is likely to happen in a particular job, course of action or activity

plant *n.* a factory or building where an industrial process takes place or a product is made

practices *n.pl.* the way people do a particular job or activity

price tag *n.* a small ticket showing the price of a product for sale

pricing *n.* the prices of a company's products or services in relation to each other and in relation to those of their competitors, and the activity of setting them

primary *adj.* main or most important

prioritise *v.* to put several tasks or problems in order of importance so that the most important ones are done first

priority *adj.* describing the thing that is more important than anything else, and that needs attention first

priority *n.* something that is considered more important or needing more attention than anything else and is therefore dealt with first

process *n.* a series of actions taken to perform a particular task or achieve a particular result

produce *n.* food that has been grown on the land or produced in large quantities, using farming methods

produce *v.* to make or grow something in large quantities to be sold

production *n.* the process of making or growing things to be sold as products, usually in large quantities

> **production process** a method used for making something on a large scale in a factory

profitability *n.* the state of producing a profit, or the degree to which an activity or company is profitable

progressive *adj.* supporting new or modern ideas, methods, etc.

purchase price *n.* the price it costs to buy something

put back *v.* to put something in the position it was before

Q

quality controls *n.pl.* a system of keeping high standards in manufactured products by planning carefully, checking and making necessary improvements

quick-response logistics *n.* organising the supply of goods and materials so that things are done very quickly

R

ramp up *v.* to increase or make something increase in amount

ratings *n.pl.* a level on a scale that shows how good, important or popular something or someone is

ration *v.* to control the supply of something so that people are allowed only a fixed amount

raw material *n.* a natural or basic substance that is used to make something in an industrial process

recycling *n.* putting used objects or materials through a special process, so that they can be used again

reduce *v.* to make something less or smaller in price, amount or size

reduction *n.* when prices, costs, etc. become lower or are made lower

reefer *n.* a refrigerated container for transporting fresh fruit and vegetables

refrigerated *adj.* when something such as food or liquid is made cold in a refrigerator in order to preserve it

regulate *v.* to control something by means of rules or laws

regulation *n.* an official rule or order

relationships *n.pl.* the way in which people and companies that are working together behave towards each other

relocate *v.* If a company *relocates* or is *relocated*, it moves to a different place.

replacement *n.* a product, piece of equipment or company that takes the place of the one currently being used

replenish *v.* to make something full again by adding new supplies to replace those that have been used

replenishment *n.* making something full again (see **replenish**)

reschedule *v.* to arrange a new time or date for an event

respond *v.* to react to something that has happened

restock *v.* to replace something that has been used with new supplies

retailer *n.* a business that sells goods directly to the public

review *v.* to examine and consider a process carefully to see if it can be improved

reviewing *n.* when a situation or process is examined and considered carefully to see if it can be improved

RFID (radio frequency identification) *n.* an electronic device used for identifying something

risk *n.* the possibility that something may be lost, harmed or damaged, or that something bad, unpleasant or dangerous may happen

risk monitoring *n.* checking in case something bad may happen

road miles *n.pl.* the distance travelled by trucks when making deliveries

run out *v.* to use all of something and not have any left

S

satellite warehouse *n.* smaller warehouse used in conjunction with a large warehouse

scarce *adj.* If something is *scarce*, there is not very much of it.

second-tier supplier *n.* a company that sells and delivers materials or goods to a first-tier or primary supplier

sector *n.* a particular area of activity or industry

secure *v.* to get something you need after a lot of effort

sell-by date *n.* the last date that a product, especially food, should be sold

sell-out *n.* when all products have sold so well there are none left

set up *v.* to start a company, organisation, system, etc.

shelf-life *n.* the length of time that a product, especially food, can be kept in a shop before it becomes too old to sell or use

shift *v.* to move (something)

shift *n.* a change in the way people think about something, in the way something is done, etc.

ship *v.* to send goods by road, rail or air

shipment *n.* a load of goods that are sent from one place to another; the process of sending goods from one place to another

shipper *n.* a company that sends goods by ship, road, rail or air

shortage *n.* a situation in which there is not enough of something that people need or want

shortfall *n.* a difference between the amount that you have and the larger amount you need or expect

simplify *v.* to make something easier or less complicated

single-source *v.* to buy materials or components from only one supplier

site *n.* a place where something has been or will be built

siting *n.* placing or building something in a particular area

smart (technology) *adj.* very advanced, usually using computers

sophistication *n.* when something is advanced in design

sort *v.* to arrange things in groups according to their type

source *n.* a place or company that you get something from

source *v.* to get materials, parts or products from a particular place

sourcing *n.* the activity of getting supplies of goods, especially ones that are used to make other goods

specification *n.* a detailed description of how something should be designed or made

specify *v.* to state something, giving exact measurements, instructions, etc.

speed up *v.* to make something move or happen faster

split *v.* to divide or separate something into different parts

spot check *n.* a check on particular things or people from a group, done without warning

state-owned *adj.* A *state-owned* industry or company is owned by the government.

static *adj.* not moving, changing or developing

status *n.* **1** importance that people give to something or someone **2** a situation at a particular time, as in the exact position of an order or a delivery

steaming speed *n.* the speed at which a ship travels

step up *v.* to increase something

stock allocation *n.* the decision to which shops to send goods

stock level *n.* the quantity of goods to keep in a shop

stock *n.* the goods that a business has for sale at a particular time

stock-out *n.* a situation in which a company has no more examples of a particular item available

store *n.* a large shop (Am.E.)

store *v.* to put things somewhere and keep them until you need them

strategic partnership *n.* a relationship between companies or organisations that work together for a special purpose

strategy *n.* a plan or series of plans for achieving an aim, especially success in business or the best way for an organisation to develop in the future

streamline *v.* to make something such as a business or organisation work more simply and effectively

strengthen *v.* to become stronger; to make somebody/something stronger

strict *adj.* Strict rules or conditions must be obeyed completely.

subcontract *v.* to pay a person or company to do some of the work that you have been given a contract to do

subcontractor *n.* a person or company who does part of the work given to another person or company

subsidiary *n.* a company that is at least half-owned by another company

supplier *n.* a company that provides raw materials, components or finished products to other companies

supplier base *n.* the number of companies that supply a bigger company (also **supply base**)

supply *n.* **1** the act of providing something **2** an amount of something that is provided or available to be used

>**supply chain** the whole series of processes, companies, places, etc. that are involved in making, selling and delivering a product. The *supply chain* includes the supply of raw materials and parts and the processes of manufacturing, storing and transporting the product to the customer.

supply *v.* to provide raw materials, goods or services to customers, especially regularly and over a long period of time

survive *v.* If a business *survives*, it manages to continue operating, even though it is in a very difficult situation.

sustainability *n.* using natural energy in a way that does not harm the environment

sustainable *adj.* involving the use of natural energy in a way that does not harm the environment

switch *v.* to change from doing or using one thing to doing or using another

T

tag *n.* an electronic device that is attached to something so that it can be checked (see **RFID**)

target *n.* a result such as a total or an amount that a business tries to achieve

technology partner *n.* a company which works with another company to supply technical services

test *v.* to use something for a short time to see if it works properly

third party *n.* a company, organisation or person that is involved in a situation in addition to the two main people or groups involved

threat *n.* the possibility that something very bad will happen

tie up *v.* to use money for something so that it is not easily available to be used for anything else

tier-one supplier *n.* a company that provides good or services direct to its customer, rather than indirectly through another company (also **primary supplier**)

time sensitive *adj.* when doing something quickly is very important

timeliness *n.* doing something at the right time

timely *adj.* done or happening at the most suitable time

tipping point *n.* the moment when one particular result of a process becomes the most likely one, after a period when the result was not sure

top-line *n.* the amount of money that a company receives from sales

total landed cost *n.* the full cost of transporting goods, including all taxes and transport costs

toxic *adj.* containing poison, or caused by poisonous substances

trade off *n.* the act of balancing two things that you need but which are opposed to each other

traffic *n.* the vehicles that are on a road at a particular time

transit *n.* the process of being moved or carried from one place to another

>**transit time** time needed to transport goods from one place to another

transition *n.* the act or process of changing from one state or form to another

transport *v.* to take goods or people from one place to another by rail, air, ship, etc.

transport *n.* a system for carrying passengers or goods from one place to another

>**transport network** a system of roads, railways and shipping routes that are connected to each other

turnover *n.* the rate at which workers leave an organisation and are replaced by others

U

uncover *v.* to find out about something that has been kept secret

V

vehicle *n.* a car, bus, etc.

vendor *n.* a company or person that sells something (also **supplier**)

vertically integrated *adj.* when a company controls all the different stages in making and selling a particular product

viable *adj.* able to be done, or worth doing

virtual enterprise *n.* a company that works with many other companies as subcontractors, so that it gives the appearance of being much bigger than it really is

visibility *n.* how easily something can be seen or noticed

visible *adj.* An effect that is *visible* is great enough to be noticed.

W

wage inflation *n.* increase in people's pay

warehouse *n.* a large building used for storing goods in large quantities, especially before they are sent to shops to be sold

wave power *n.* energy provided by the movement of the sea

wholly owned *adj.* when a company is owned completely by another company

widespread *adj.* existing or happening in many places or situations

withhold *v.* to refuse to let someone have something

working capital *n.* money used by a business to carry on production and keep trading, for example to pay employees and suppliers before money is received for goods sold

working conditions *n.pl.* the circumstances or situation in which people work